Why Am I Here?
Believe In Your Truth

Maureen G. Kayata

WWW.Connections.Solutions

Library of Congress Cataloging –in-Publication Data
Under the original title: - And Now I Can See – Believe
In Yourself

Cover Photo: Maureen G. Kayata

Peases Point Mattapoisett MA

Co-published by Publlissimo and Connections

Publish Date – April 25, 2016

ISBN: 10: 978-0692701109
ISBN-13: 978-0692701102

iv

DEDICATION

This book is dedicated to my sister, Laurie Ann, who is one of the kindest, gentlest, and most thoughtful souls that I have ever encountered

Laurie, you are so creative and talented. You have more energy and enthusiasm in one day than most people do in a year. I love your creativity and artistic abilities. You have changed the lives of so many children throughout your years of teaching. You have the ability to see the unique qualities in all children, no matter where they come from or how they behave. You are the "one person", the life changer. You are the HOPE.

It only takes one person to change another person's life. You have changed my life. You are my #1 supporter and confidant. You believe in me even when I don't believe in myself. You are my Angel. Someday you will be completely understood and appreciated for who you are. I would like that day to be today. I wish you all the success and happiness in all of your life dreams. You have helped me to make my dreams come true and now it is your turn! Thank you for all that you do in this world. I love you, Laurie!

ACKNOWLEDGMENTS

To my husband, David, for always being there, believing in me and supporting me.

To my dear friend, Meredith Poulten, for constantly encouraging me and helping me to understand the importance of this work.

To my sweet cousin, Susan Cipollaro, for being my lifeline. You saved me on more occasions than you know.

TABLE OF CONTENTS

FOREWORD

I was asked to write this book by someone I have never met. It is actually pretty amazing, since when I was asked to write this book, the person was no longer here on Earth. This is still mind blowing, even to me. His name is Jonathan. I will tell you his story in the first chapter. This is a book to tell all of "their" stories; in "their" own words. These are the stories of the souls that abruptly departed this Earth as a way to find peace, solitude, a missing answer, or to end their pain. Jonathan needed my help. He had a message he wanted to share with me. I wasn't willing to listen. He kept persisting until finally I said "OK! What is it that you have to tell me?" He revealed that I must write this book to tell the stories of all the suicide victims. I remember him saying "We need you to be our voice, tell our story, the story that we couldn't speak ourselves while we were here on Earth." I asked him "Why me?" He answered, "Because you do not judge us and you are a great listener." I made a promise that day in April 2013, and here is the result of that promise.

As far back as I can remember I started to receive downloads. I describe a download as a "message" that comes in unexpectedly. This would happen to me frequently, whether in a business meeting, having coffee with a friend, or when I first wake up in the morning.

Sometimes it happens in a dream, but most of these messages come when I am fully awake. I don't ask for these messages, they just come.

It took me a long time to understand what to do with this information. When should I give a message and when shouldn't I?

I am a very intuitive person. That is something I do not tell many people. It is something I did not even know about myself for many years. Of course, I was aware I was different. I knew from a very early age that I could see and hear things that other people around me could not see or hear. I also knew that I should never reveal this information to anyone in my life. It was my little secret. I knew it wasn't safe to reveal the secret of this gift to anyone. Instead, I tried my hardest to ignore these gifts I was born with so I could be like everyone else. That didn't work and it made things more difficult for me.

I can remember being in the first grade and knowing that my teacher was a very dishonest, mean, and fake person. I was only six years old. She was a catholic nun. My private school teachings did not teach me to judge like this. It didn't make sense to me. I knew I should not have these thoughts about my teacher, but I did. She would validate my feelings on a daily basis. When the principal came into our classroom my first grade teacher would be very gentle and kind. When the principal left the room my teacher would be very hateful and mean. She would go through the garbage after lunch and if she found any food that was thrown away she would wait until someone admitted to throwing it away and then she would make them eat it in front of the whole class. The days that no one would admit to throwing away their lunch our whole class would be punished for the rest of that day. I remember never feeling safe in her presence. I understood that this woman was very unhappy and was taking out her own internal rage and pain on the children in her class. I never said a word to anyone about these thoughts or feelings. I knew that if I kept very quiet and

2

stayed out of her path of destruction that I would be OK. She died shortly after that. I remember thinking she probably died because she was so filled with self-hatred and anger. I do not think this is a normal thought for a little six year old to have. She was less than 30 years old at the time of her death.

I have spent countless years trying to hide, ignore, and forget about my gifts. I have concluded that this is not possible, so I am working on embracing my gifts and I have decided to use them to help others. That is why I have agreed to write this book. I have felt the pain of so many of my clients who come to get a message from their deceased loved ones. The suicide victim family sessions are the most painful. That is why when Jonathan pleaded with me to write this book, I understood I was being called to an important life purpose and I knew I had to tell you "their" stories in their own words.

The Beginning of The Story:

L et me tell you how I met Jonathan. I have a full time job. As I mentioned, not many people know that I am an intuitive person, and definitely not at my day job.

I received a call from a client who I had met once about a year earlier. She wanted me to come to "clear" her house. Clearing a house entails getting rid of any stuck energy and replacing it with pure clean unconditional love. This is a very simple way to explain a very complex process. There are different methods you can use to do this. No matter which method you decide to use, it is very exhausting work. You always have to make sure you protect yourself and pray for assistance from the other side prior to doing this work. For me, that entails asking God, Jesus, the Holy Spirit, and Mother Mary to protect, assist, and guide me. I ask that the outcome will be for the highest and best of all parties involved. Then I usually ask if there are any saints and angels available to assist me. I clear my own home weekly but I do not typically go to other people's homes to clear their space.

The client that contacted me stated that she was desperate for me to come to clear her home. She felt there was a spirit in her home that was disturbing her family and their home life. Her two children ages 16 and 13 would no longer sleep in their own bedrooms. This is not something I typically do for other people. This is not something that I wanted to do. I tried to refer her to someone else. I told her I wasn't available for several weeks. I told her my fee, which was very large. She kept insisting she wanted to hire me. She lived an hour from me and I really did not want to do this.

I called a friend of mine named John. John is a Police Chief whom I have done a lot of spiritual work for in the past. He too is a spiritual practitioner and we often network our resources. I called John and explained the situation to him, the distance, and the time restrictions on my already overloaded schedule, the fact that I wasn't comfortable, how I tried to refer this client to someone else, etc. I thought for sure John would say don't do it. Instead, I remember being shocked when I heard John say, "They want you, just be the light and go help these people." Seriously? I don't even really know this family and I am driving an hour away to clear the energy in their home, which is not something I am comfortable doing. John repeated, "They want you. You called to ask me my opinion and I think you should do it, just be the light." It was that message that gave me the courage to go. I was so scared for so many reasons. What if I couldn't do this? What if this spirit or whatever this was follows me home? What if this is sacrilegious? I heard my friend John's words in my mind again, "just be the light." I called the family the next day and told them I would come to clear their home. They were very grateful.

It was a Friday night in April. I worked a full day and headed to the client's home right after leaving work. I remember my heart pounding, thinking, what if the clearing doesn't work? What if I can't get this spirit to leave? What if the spirit can feel my fear? I knew then that I wasn't connected to my divine guidance so I started to pray and asked to be wrapped in a protective shield. As I entered into my client's town I felt a spirit with me. Even though I am an intuitive person I don't like it when a spirit just shows up. I have rules and boundaries and I insist that the spiritual realm follows them.

Rule #1: Do not try to speak to me if you have not crossed into the light.

Rule #2: Do not ask me to approach your family members with messages. If you want me to speak to your family members to give them a message then you have to get them to come and see me.

I don't believe in freaking people out by giving them random messages from their deceased loved ones. I consider it disrespectful. Everyone grieves differently and I think you have to respect that at the highest level.

This spirit was a male and was in the passenger seat of my car. I knew I was protected because I had just prayed, but I still felt unsettled. I heard him say, "I have to talk to you." When I communicate with spirits on the other side I do so telepathically. So using this method, I said, "No, I am not available to speak with you right now and I have rules." He replied, "Yes, I am aware of your rules." I knew this man had hung himself and I knew he had not crossed to the light, so I was not about to engage in a conversation with him. I was getting closer to my client's house so I just ignored him and continued to drive. This type of encounter has only happened to me a few times and I really don't like it. I felt invaded.

As I approached my client's house I could feel my belly doing flips. I had to really tap into my faith and let God take over and guide me. I forgot all about the man in my car and entered into my client's home. She pointed out that the main issue was in one of the bedrooms to the right at the end of the hallway and right outside that bedroom into the hallway.

I connected with God, Jesus, The Holy Spirit, and Mother Mary. I asked any angels, saints, ascended masters, and deceased loved ones who were available to assist me, to please come through. I saw a bright light and a feeling of unconditional love surround me. I felt a sense of strength and peace immediately, so I knew it was safe to begin. I went into the bedroom at the end of the hallway to the right. I immediately felt a man who had taken his own life by hanging himself. When I do my work I am so hyper focused I never even thought about the encounter I had with the man I felt in my car just a few minutes earlier. This man in the bedroom pretty much refused to leave. I spent a good amount of time in there with him. I used holy water, prayed, used sage, etc. Nothing I did seemed to work. This man refused to leave. He just kept saying over and over again "I have to talk to you." The great thing about having the gift of telepathic communication is that I could answer this spirit without my client knowing that he was there. She already looked so scared so I didn't want to bring any more fear into the situation. I answered him with my usual response, " I have rules and I can't talk to you because you haven't crossed into the light."

He insisted again. I answered him by saying, "I can tell that you haven't crossed into the light, so NO!" He kept saying, "I have something important to tell you." I said, "No, I don't receive downloaded messages from spirits that have not crossed into the light." He insisted that his message was very important for me to hear. I said, "No, I have rules and I am not willing to break them or listen to you right now, you need to leave this house and go to the light." He still refused to leave.

I knew I had to move to the other rooms or I would never be able to finish all of the work we had to complete. I was already feeling drained from my encounter with him. I turned to my client and told her that I would have to clear the rest of the house and then return to the bedroom to clear it again. This spirit would not leave and I didn't want to alarm the client. The rest of the home clearing went smoothly, but I knew that spirit was still in the first bedroom and I had to try to get him to move on. I returned to the first bedroom and started to clear the energy again. This man was very resistant to leaving this home. I had never encountered this before. He just kept repeating over and over again "I have to talk to you, I have something very important to tell you." The main reason I will not communicate with a spirit that has not crossed is because I have no idea if the information they give me is from the divine source or light. If a spirit is communicating from the light I have a different kind of feeling and I know their message is protected. This time I didn't respond to his pleading. I just stated in a very firm telepathic voice, "You cannot stay in this home, it is not yours and this family deserves to live in a peaceful home." I showed him a beautiful bench right outside of Heaven's gate and said, "You do not have to cross if you do not want to, but you cannot stay here in this home. This home belongs to this family. You can go sit on that beautiful bench and choose any one from the spirit world to sit with you until you are ready to go to the light, but you cannot stay here." It worked. I couldn't believe it! He left the house! My work was done and I finally got to go home after a very long and draining day.

I left my client's house and got into my car to drive home. I wasn't even a mile away from her home when I heard the same man speak to me from the passenger seat in my car. It startled me as this had never happen to me before. I was a little scared, but knew I was protected. I asked him why he was in my car and I told him he was not coming to my house with me. I was regretting my decision to do this work already. As I said, it is not something I enjoy doing. He said he needed to speak with me. This is the same thing he kept repeating over and over in the house. I started to repeat my rules, "I do not communicate with..." He cut me off and said, "Yes I am well aware of your rules. I have been following you for a very long time." Now I was really getting nervous. Then I heard him say, "Please Maureen, I just have one thing to tell you. It is so important and it will change your life forever." My mind was whirling; he knew my name and had been following me? I was trying to think of what to do next. I heard him say, "Maureen, if you listen to me and let me just tell you this one thing then I promise that I will cross into the light." I asked him how I knew I could trust him. What if he gave me his message and then followed me all of the way home? Then I realized, it is an honor to help someone to cross into the light. I prayed to God, Jesus, Mother Mary, and the Holy Spirit. I felt a sense of peace come over me and knew this man was telling me the truth. I asked him, "Are you telling me the truth? Will you cross into the light if I let you tell me your one message?" He said, "Yes, Maureen, I promise. If you let me tell you the message I will cross into the light." Believe it or not, even though this was scary for me, when this man spoke to me he was so gentle and kind. I could tell he had a pure heart. "Promise." I said, "OK give me your message."

The next thing I heard him say was "Maureen, please write a book." My reply was "What? That is your big message to me? Asking me to write a book? I have heard that message from many other people before you, this is not something new." Then I heard him repeat, "Maureen, please write a book and speak for us! Tell our stories. Let us speak through you." I felt myself get completely emotional. "You want me to speak for you? Who?" He responded, "For all of us, the suicide victims, we need to tell our stories, we need to be heard, we want you to speak for us, we will speak through you in this book." I was near tears. I could barely whisper, so I asked him, "Why me?" I heard him say, "Because you don't judge us, you listen and we trust you." I said, "OK I will write the book, I will tell your stories." I heard him say, "You promise?" I answered him, "Yes, I promise, I will do it. I will write the book." Then I heard him say, "OK I will cross now. Once I cross you will channel messages for my family, right?" I responded with, "Yes, but you will have to get them to come to me, that is my rule, I do not give messages unless the family comes to see me." I heard him say, "Yes, I know all about your rules. I have been following you for a very long time. Don't worry, I will get them to come to see you." I felt his spirit cross into the light and I felt an amazing sense of peace and happiness.

After he left I felt myself become completely emotional. I had just made a huge promise to write a book so that the suicide victims could tell their stories. I cried all the way home. I was completely overwhelmed and honored at the same time. I can't believe they chose me. Why me? I knew this book would change my life forever, but I knew I had to commit to the promise I just made. Then I wondered, how is this going to work? Who will come to me? I heard this same man's voice in a distance, "Don't worry Maureen, they are lined up waiting to speak to you. They will come, just write the book."

His name is Jonathan, and he has the most gentle and beautiful soul. His family came to me the very next day after my encounter with Jonathan. I did not know it was his family, not right away. I had booked the appointment a month earlier. You probably think that when I do this work all of the pieces connect right away. This is rarely the case. It is usually the spirit world that has to point these connections out to me.

CHAPTER I
Jonathan's Story

Hello, my name is Jonathan. I hung myself. I didn't know what else to do. I was born with biblical knowledge constantly running through my mind. I had verses from the Bible repeating through my head and mind every minute of every day. I felt like Moses. I was never understood on this Earth. Some people classified me as having "mental illness." I felt my father's disapproval of me at a very young age. I just wanted him to accept and love me for who I was. It wasn't my fault I was born this way. He wanted me to play sports. I had no interest in playing sports and I had no talent for sports. I was an intellect. I knew his thoughts. I knew when he would think, "Why can't you just be normal like your brother?" Even my brother learned to ignore me and pretend I wasn't there. I just wanted to be accepted for who I was and I wanted to fit in. If your own family can't accept you then what chance do you have? It is hard when you have a mind that works faster than your body. You have thousands of thoughts scrolling through your mind that you know you cannot express to anyone here on Earth. You understand at a very young age that you are different. The hardest part of my "gift" was that I knew what others were thinking of me even if they didn't say it. I could hear their thoughts in my mind. I could hear them as clear as you hear words coming out of someone's mouth.

My second grade teacher didn't like me. She was mean to me. Her thoughts were absolutely hateful. It is tough to swallow this every day, especially as a seven year old. The worst part of it was when the other kids would pick up on how much my teacher disliked me. That is when the bullying started; followed by the sneering, whispering, and the mean notes. This is when I really started to feel bad about myself. When I was home I felt my dad's disapproval and when I was at school I felt my teacher's disapproval. I learned to be really quiet. I tried to become invisible; because of this, mixed with the thousands of negative thoughts scrolling through my mind, I began to feel very lonely and sad. I began to accept other people's thoughts as my own. I started to hate myself and so my vicious cycle began.

I, personally, never felt like I belonged here on Earth. I never felt like I belonged anywhere. The depression grew deep within me. I started separating myself as much as I could. Layer by layer I removed myself until my mind felt like my only friend. Nothing brings you joy or excitement. You search and search but you can't see any purpose or any joy in your life. I thought about killing myself for a long time. I would be sitting in a crowd of people either at school or at a family gathering and while I watched the others around me laugh and talk, I would think, "I could disappear right now and no one would notice." The one thing that stops you from ending your life is the fear that things will continue exactly as they are even after your life ends. That is worse than anything because that means there is no end to the way you are feeling. I felt trapped. I felt there was no way out. The pain I felt was in my throat. This pain came from not being able to express myself.

I know now that the thoughts came from my mother reading the Bible to me every day while she was carrying me and all through my early childhood. I knew the Bible inside and out probably before I could even speak. I didn't always understand it but I knew the Bible was filled with fear. That is a lot to absorb as a small child. My parents were fear-based people. That same fear grew inside of me every day. Honestly, I didn't think my death would matter to anyone. I hung myself to end the pain, to kill all of the words stuck in my throat that I couldn't express. Even my death was classified as "disturbing." How sad is that?

Jonathan's Life Message:

I am not disturbed. I am very much alive and well and happy. I have learned to accept myself. This is something I found very difficult to do on Earth. My message for those still on Earth is "PLEASE DO NOT JUDGE." If I can help one child or person have a better life then I will know that I have served my purpose. This is why I needed to have this book written and published. We have a lot of information that could bring a lot of value to those still on Earth, if you will just listen and take the time to "SEE" the miracles that are right in front of you. Did you know that a miracle could happen in a second? That is right! In one tiny second you can experience a miracle that will make all of the difference in the world. One kind word can change the outcome of someone's life. Did you ever think about that? Say something kind even if you don't feel like it. Be kind and do kind things for everyone who crosses your path. Take the time to care now so you don't have to regret it later or suffer because you didn't do something or say something you knew you should have. Remember this.... It is very important.

This is what I want you to know about me. I was born with a heart full of love, as every innocent child is. It was through the years of rejection, the years of absorbing other people's negative thoughts and fears about me that I started to believe I had less and less value. Have you ever sat in solitary confinement? It is the loneliest feeling in the world. You can hear your own thoughts and the words in your head. When you are ignored by society, like you don't even exist, it is like being in solitary confinement. If you don't understand what I am saying, try sitting in a room all by yourself for several hours without speaking to anyone, or go away by yourself without interacting with anyone else for a whole weekend. You will become so lonely, so fast. After a while you will start to hear your own thoughts. These thoughts will probably be all of the other people's words and thoughts that you have absorbed and heard over the years.

When I entered into the light, which I describe as unconditional love and which you refer to as Heaven, it was pure bliss. It was pure acceptance on every level. I felt pure joy. I felt accepted. Here is a secret; it was me who had to accept me. I felt a perfectness that I had never experienced on Earth. I am here to tell you that you can experience this on Earth right now. That is the message I wanted to share with you. Each time you accept yourself or someone else, each time you send yourself or someone else a positive thought or smile you will open your heart to this blissful experience. If you do this, it will radiate through you and the people around you will notice your energy shift immediately. They will ask you what is different about you. They will know you are different, but they won't be able to figure out what you have changed. They will ask you if you changed your hair or if you lost some weight.

This shift will radiate throughout the world and others will start to follow your suit. Yes, one person can have a huge impact in this world, but not because they are famous or have a lot of money. No, these things do not change the world, but one kind word will. That is all it takes to start this shift and for you to experience this pure unconditional love that I am referring to, ONE KIND WORD. It starts with you. Thank you for letting me tell my story. Peace to all, Jonathan."

CHAPTER II
Hello my name is Matthew

I have waited a long time to tell you my story. No one really knows if I committed suicide. Was it an accident? Did I overdose on drugs and alcohol by accident? Or was it intentional? "He always seemed so happy." No, that is what you wanted to believe. My death was intentional to stop my internal pain and insecurity. I wanted to erase being different, to get rid of it. Leaving a trace of that decision would make getting over my death a lot more difficult, so I exited the safe way, or so I thought.

I was classified as "gay." I knew I was different in the first grade. I didn't think the same way that other boys did. I didn't like the same things they liked. I knew I was different. My mom knew I was different, too! I remember one time she took me to a store to get a Tonka Truck. The store was loaded with all different kinds. I didn't want one and no matter how much my mother tried to coax me and no matter how many cool things those trucks could do, I had no interest. We left the store with no truck and my mom being very upset with me. I heard her whisper under her breath, "Why can't you just be like the other boys your age?" That was the first slice to my heart. Why couldn't I just get a box of crayons in that store? That is all I really wanted. I loved to draw and create. Purple was and remains to be my favorite color (and this has nothing to do with being "gay"), but I learned to keep that a secret. I learned to keep a lot of things secret. School was tough and got even worse as I got older. When we had to play sports in gym class, it became clear that I was different. If the ball hurt someone I felt the pain. I was that sensitive. I hated the rough housing but I had to smile and pretend it was all OK.

I did not choose to be born this way. I just was. When a baby is born the parents and doctors look to make sure everything is normal. They look to make sure there are ten fingers and ten toes. "Oh and look at those beautiful eyes. He is absolutely perfect." They don't check to see if you are gay. They are just happy you arrived safe and healthy. Why can't it stay that way? Because, as you grow your differences become noticeable. There is embarrassment, questions, harassment and then more questions. How do you explain something you were born with to someone that you don't even understand yourself? Do you say, I was born this way? I know disabled people must deal with this same issue. For them it is probably even worse since their disability is noticeable right away. My difference became apparent when I started school and all of the comparisons started. In the playground one day I overheard another mother talking to my mother. She said, "My little Johnny just loves playing with Tonka Trucks." Hence why we ended up at the Tonka Truck store the very next day.

Matthew's Life Message:

It is so painful and hurtful to be different. I am smiling as I say this because now I know and understand that our creator or "GOD" intended for us to all be different. Why do you think he gave everyone in the world a unique set of fingerprints? Because we are all suppose to be different. How did we get on this "dummy" footprint of duplicating ourselves over and over again? How did we get on the path of erasing our uniqueness, our own identity of who we came to be? It comes from society shaping us and our beliefs about us. But, more importantly, it comes from our own insecurity. We don't accept ourselves, so how can others. It is not the other way around. You don't accept yourself because others accept you. No, you accept yourself and then it doesn't matter if others accept you. They don't have the decision. You do. It has to start with you. You have to accept yourself in all of your glory. Enjoy being who you are. It starts here:

Simple steps for you to follow to find your own self-acceptance and happiness:

Step #1: Be happy with who you are, embrace everything about yourself. Love your differences even more, don't try to hide them.

Step #2: Never look outside of yourself for approval. This will destroy you.

Step #3: Do what you love, start exploring this right away if you don't already know.

Step #4: Wear what you love, even if it is purple.

Step #5: Do something that makes you happy every day. Make sure whatever you choose is good for you and not self-sabotaging (that will catch up with you or kill you).

Step #6: Say a mantra or positive statement that brings you peace and hope (keep it simple). Write it down and say it ten times every day. Always return to it when you are feeling out of sorts.

Follow these simple steps and you will feel happier with yourself and happier with your life. You will draw in the right kind of relationships for you. It is OK to be different. It was meant to be this way.

My final life message is don't value other people's opinions more than you value your own. You know what is best for you.
They do not. They know what is best for them.

Thank you for letting me share my story with you, Matthew.

CHAPTER III
Hello my name is Katie

D id you know that sometimes the most seemingly unnoticed event could really rock a person's world and make them become unstable overnight? That is what happened to me. I was very popular in high school. Most people would say that I had it all. I was pretty, thin, I had a decent personality, and I came from a rich family, who lived in a nice home in a "Jones" type neighborhood. Things were good; at least they appeared to be on the outside.

My dad had a very lucrative job and my mom was happy staying at home and doing all of those little extra things like running charity events, volunteering, and serving on community committees. I have two siblings, one older and one younger. My younger sister and I fought constantly. I was active in school. I was on the track team and I was a cheerleader. My life was really quite simple. Of course when you are in your own life it never really seems simple, fun or easy.

I was never satisfied. I always wanted more or had some drama going on, mostly self-induced. My hair wasn't blond enough or long enough. I always got tangled up in my friend's problems. I wanted to be even more popular than I was. That is why when the guy who was head of the football team asked me out I was ecstatic. I remember thinking, now I can have the life that I have always wanted. I knew right away that I would do whatever it took to keep him interested. I was already dreaming of wearing his jacket to let everyone know he was mine. So of course I had to modify myself even more so that I would be perfect. I had to get him to want me. I knew this would be difficult since he had a long string of girls before me, but I was convinced that I could get him to fall in love with me and to think about me all of the time. My heart started pounding just thinking about this.

Our first date was at a pizza shop. All of his friends were there but not with us, just at the surrounding tables. I hadn't eaten for almost a whole week so that I would look perfect in my tight skinny white jeans. I wore a pink button down shirt and a sexy negligee underneath. I buttoned the shirt low to make sure he got a glimpse of what he could have. I knew I had to make him want me. I wore my best perfume and pumps to make my legs look extra-long and thin. I remember walking into the pizza shop and I could see his friend drooling over me. One guy in particular could not take his eyes off of me. The guy I was with barely even noticed how much trouble I had gone through to look this good. He did notice my negligee though. I caught him looking down my shirt several times. I knew exactly how to play this game. I would let my hair fall to cover what he wanted to see and after about five minutes I would flip my head back so my hair would go behind my shoulder so he could get a glimpse of me. I wanted to drive him crazy. The whole time, I could see his friend with the blond hair and big blue eyes behind him just staring at me. I could almost read his mind, and I knew that he wanted to be with me in the worst way. This kind of made up for the fact that my own date only noticed one part of me. I don't even think he looked into my eyes. So I would glance at his friend's eyes just to get a little rush and then flip my hair so my date could get a little glimpse of me. I knew as soon as we hit the car he would try to get all over me. This would be the hard part. Pretending I wasn't ready and asking him to drive me home, only allowing him to kiss me on the cheek before saying goodnight to me. I could see the frustration, almost anger in his eyes. This was mixed with some confusion, I could hear him thinking "but I always get what I want." Yeah, well, this time I am going to get what I want. I want to be the most popular girl in school. I want to wear your letter jacket. I want every one of your friends to crave me and when I am good and ready and I think you are about to bust at the seams, I will give in to you and leave you craving me even more than you have ever craved another human being on this Earth before. That was my plan.

I wanted people to remember who I was in high school. I wanted to be the one. It is actually funny to hear the words I am speaking right now. I was so shallow, to think that being popular in high school would help to determine who I was and the success I would have in my life. That is craziness! But you know what, my plan worked. Those people all remember me and they will never forget me. Even "you" will never forget me. Your life was going to change forever too! Every time you got frustrated and thought about dumping me because you were tired of waiting to get what you wanted, one of your friends would jump in and make a statement like "Wow! I would die to go out with a girl like that." You didn't have the heart or should I say you didn't have the courage to tell them that you weren't getting anything from me. You were afraid they would think less of you. You were afraid they would come after me and try to win me over before you could. It was just a game for you. You were the shallow one.

This went on for a few months until one night after winning your football game you asked me to meet you on the field after you showered and changed. The whole place had cleared out. It was a beautiful night. You started to actually treat me like a girlfriend and I knew I had to make my move or I would risk you moving on to someone else. You actually thought I was a virgin. I was very good at playing innocent and the victim. I loved all of the attention I would get. Even my own family was completely taken with you. I already had your jacket and that is what kept me warm that night as I waited for you. That was the night I gave you exactly what you wanted. It happened right there under the bleachers. It sounds so cliché. I whispered I was scared even though the truth is I couldn't wait to make you want me even more and gain more power and control over you, really over my own life. It was over so quickly I barely had time to react. We drove home in silence, as I had to play the victim role. You kissed me hard that night almost like you were thanking me for giving you the gift you had been waiting for and because I made you wait so long I knew you would be back for more.

When your friends saw the change in the look of your eyes, they thought you had fallen in love. They didn't know it was because you finally got what you had wanted ever since that very first night two months earlier. The funny thing was, now you actually looked at me. Now you almost became a little possessive as if no one else was going to have me, you thought you were the only one. I was the most popular girl in school.

My family couldn't get over how much I was maturing. No one realized it was all a lie. I was driven by insecurity. I had to be popular so everyone would like me. So everyone would notice me. I loved to be the center of attention, but in a quiet way. I want you to look at me, crave me, and desire me, but I don't want to have to talk a lot or tell you what I am really thinking. If you knew half of what I was thinking I wouldn't be popular at all. Even though I got what I wanted I was always feeling kind of depressed. I would take diet pills like candy to decrease my appetite so that my body could be as skinny as possible. So I could play my role well.

Two months into this charade I found out I was pregnant. Pregnant! That would mean you would dump me, I knew you didn't actually love me or care about me. You just possessed me. I could tell because you never spent time looking into my eyes. Your eyes were always attempting to get down my shirt or down my pants. Our dates were always quick because you had one thing on your mind to accomplish and that was to get me to fuck you. It wasn't even enjoyable. You never took your time. It was quick and fast. Wam, bam thank you mam. You never asked me anything or talk to me afterwards. You never even held me; you just pulled up your pants and said OK let's get going. Everything on the outside looked so perfect. Everything on the inside was so wrong. That is why when I found out I was pregnant I knew what I had to do.

My dad is a physician. He would kill me when he found out. How many lectures did I get about this exact thing? I couldn't get an abortion, I knew all about the complications with that too, plus, what if my dad found out? That would be even worse. He knew everyone. I knew you would leave me and move on to the next pretty girl. This is a funny statement since you were never with me to begin with. I knew when people found out I was pregnant I would be tainted. No one would want me. No one would look at me the same way ever again. My mom would just cry and ask herself over and over again where she went wrong. She put everything she had into raising our family.

My little sister, the one that I fought with constantly, would probably make fun of me and enjoy watching me get fat. My older brother would probably never look at me again. He had warned me over and over about you. Of course I didn't listen to him. I was not a good listener. I was defiant and had my own agenda and my own way of doing things. All I could hear was my own loud voice in my mind saying, "Boy you really screwed up this time and you better take care of this." I would be ridiculed at school. I saw what happened to girls who got pregnant at school.

What a mess I made out of my life. I couldn't see a clear way out. I knew I had to end my life. I had to end the embarrassment, the shame, and the insecurity of constantly hating myself every day. That is why I decided to end my life. I had to take care of this before anyone knew I was pregnant.

I did take care of it. I hung myself. I wanted to take pills and take the easy way out. I knew if I did that, they would test what was in my stomach and they would find out that I was pregnant. I did not want anyone to find out about my pregnancy. I didn't want to bring any shame brought to my family.

My plan worked. My family was so distraught and devastated that they never even thought about doing an autopsy. Not even my dad, the doctor. When people are in shock they don't think clearly. I took my life and my baby daughter's life. I got to meet her and she would have been a beautiful delightful child who would have brought my family and me so much joy. She has blond hair with long bouncy ringlets and blue eyes. She has one of those laughs that are so contagious that you think about it even when you are not with her. She has forgiven me for my decision. I could have had this wonderful child in my life for a very long time. My family would have gotten over the shock of my pregnancy in no time at all. This would have healed my relationship with my sister because she would have stood by my side every step of the way. Her and my baby daughter would have been inseparable.

Katie's Life Message:

I can't take back my decision to end my life, but I am hoping to help one person to make a different choice. It started with me wanting to be like everyone else. I think that is funny now as I was supposed to be exactly like I was, but I couldn't comprehend that and I certainly couldn't get that when I was on Earth.

My decisions on Earth would have affected me for the rest of my life. That one life changing decision, had I made a different choice, would have brought me, and my family countless years of joy and goodness. Everything would have worked out for the best. Instead, I chose the easy cowardly route out and to this day it has left my family feeling helpless and aimless. I watch their individual pain and it is unbearable.

My dad cannot understand how he didn't see the signs of depression when he helps countless people with this same issue every year. "Dad, there was no depression. I was reckless and then I chose to be more reckless. You didn't miss anything."

My little sister now hates herself thinking that all of the mean things she said to me are what caused me to take my own life. "Kali, no! The things you said to me were all true and I needed to hear them. Plus, I was the one who should have been setting an example for you. I did a terrible job with that."

My brother John is now depressed because he feels he couldn't protect me. He thinks he wasn't there for me enough. "John, you were there for me all the time and I appreciate everything you did for me. You were right about my choices. I just didn't want to listen to you or hear you."

My mom, well I can't even talk about my mom. Here is a woman who dedicated most of her adult life to caring for her family in the very best way she knew how. Then she continually helped others to set a legacy for my siblings and me. "Mom, you are the kindest, warmest, best mom in the whole world. You are the epitome of what a human should be. You taught us so well on how to treat others. Honestly mom, if I had stuck it out. I would have been just like you." To all of my family, friends, teachers, coaches... I am sorry for my careless and reckless decisions. Please value your life every day and know that there is always a different choice right around the corner. Just decide one day at a time. Your life is meant to be happy and fulfilling. You can make a better choice than I did. You are worth it! Be someone and do something positive with your life. Be what you were meant to be. How will you ever know if you don't stick it out? Katie

CHAPTER IV
Hello, my name is L.

I was murdered in a massacre. Did you know the only difference between people who takes their own life and people who take another's life is how they direct their anger? The person who takes his own life directs all of his anger, disappointments, and insecurities inward, toward himself. A person who takes another person's life directs all of his anger, disappointments, and hatred outward, toward the person or persons he kills. They both go through similar steps to get there. Society tries their best to analyze this after the fact but you can't analyze this. It is impossible to understand what is going through a person's brain when they make the decision to end a life. It doesn't just happen; it is a buildup of events and disappointments over time.

The day I was killed, my day started out perfect. I woke up extra early and looked out the window. I could tell it was cold just by looking out the window, but I could feel this was going to be an extra special day. It felt like everything was perfect. I met the man of my dreams. I had finally landed a more permanent job doing what I loved. I had an amazing support system of family and friends that loved and accepted me. I finally felt that I loved myself. I felt perfect for the first time in my life. What an amazing feeling that is.

I am going to tell you how I got here. It was the children. I had landed a job where I got to be with beautiful children every day. They love themselves so much at that young age. They are so innocent.

Everything about them is honest and pure. They don't hold anything back. They share their every thought and event in their lives. Every day felt like a miracle to me. I loved the sound of their voices. I loved listening to their stories. I loved how I was the teacher, but every day when I came home to see my family I would tell them how these young small children were teaching me. That was it; every day I would learn something new from these innocent souls. They made me laugh and they made me cry. I knew this is what I was supposed to do with the rest of my life and I knew that someday I would want to have children of my own. I did, I got to experience what it is what like to have children of my own that very day.

I went through my usual morning routine of getting ready and for some strange reason I couldn't wait to get to school that day. It was like there was something special that was going to happen even though I knew there was nothing special planned on the calendar. It was a Friday so maybe that was it. Friday always seemed extra special anyway. The kids always had more energy on Fridays. I guess everyone did.

I arrived at the school a little earlier that day. I remember being in the classroom noticing how quiet it was and realizing that I did not like it. I like the noise and the energy of the children, their feet shuffling, their pencils dropping, their coughs and their laughs. I loved it all, every minute of it. I knew I was where I was supposed to be. This felt like home to me, the home of my soul. It was the Christmas season but I couldn't stop thinking about Valentine's Day. I was already thinking about a special project we could do together. I was so lost in my own thoughts that I didn't even hear the bell ring. The kids came flocking into the room and it felt surreal. I noticed how beautiful they looked to me that day. One little girl with blonde hair just smiled at me, it melted my heart. I remember whispering under my breath. "I am the luckiest person on Earth."

We went through our usual morning routine and we were just about ready to get settled into the day when I heard someone yelling. I knew what I had to do. It was probably just another drill about school safety. I didn't panic; I just simply walked to the door and locked it. I went into my quiet whisper voice and told the children we had to move to the back of the classroom. My whisper voice always got their attention and they always listened. As we moved to the back of the room I heard what sounded like a popping noise. I felt a warm sensation pass down through me from the top of my head to the bottom of my feet. I realized at that moment that this wasn't a drill. I knew I had to get the children further back and huddled so I could protect them. I told them we were going to play a game that we had never played before but that it had to be done in total silence. We had to get as close to each other as we could and stay as quiet as we could. I could see the fear in their eyes and I knew I had to let go of my own fear or they would sense it and my plan would not work. I wanted to protect them and I knew I had to.

One little girl started to cry softly. We were huddled tightly in a small circle, almost in a ball. I kept whispering, "It is going to be OK" I could barely hear her whisper but then I heard her say, "but I have to go to the bathroom." She couldn't move, she was so tightly woven into our "circle of love." That is what I told the children, "We are going to play a new game called "Circle of Love." You have to be extra extra quiet and we have to be extra extra close so we can feel each other's love and the love of the angels and God surrounding us." They did exactly what I told them too. The little girl softly crying was the only sound in the room. I told her, "its OK honey just go to the bathroom right here, it will be OK You have to trust me". The next thing I heard was the sound of her peeing right there on the floor. None of the other children moved or said a word. You couldn't even smell the urine. She stopped crying. I told the children "we must remain very very quiet so that you can hear a song I am going to whisper to you ever so softly. I whispered the song, "Somewhere Over the Rainbow." It was the newer version of the song with the ukulele that I was thinking about. There wasn't a sound, they just kept their heads down and listened. As I whispered this song, something I have never whispered in my life, I saw a soft white light that entered the room and surrounded our "Circle of Love." It was like a wispy soft light that felt very warm like a very soft sun. There was such a sense of peace and happiness. We were two and one half to three feet above the circle still in the "Circle of Love," but as I looked up there were just beautiful smiles on the children's faces. I have never felt so much love and peace in my life. At that moment I realized that this is what it feels like to be a mother. This is what unconditional love feels like. I couldn't wait to get home to tell my family about this incredibly beautiful experience. I didn't think they would even believe me. I couldn't even believe what was happening myself. Then I understood an even deeper meaning. This is what it feels like to be in God's love. That is what the "Circle of Love" is truly about. We were all experiencing pure sweet unconditional love and it was the most amazing feeling I have ever experienced in my life. It was a deep soul changing experience. The kind you can't explain in human words. The kind that you know when you do try to explain it no one will really be able to understand what you are speaking about. I didn't care. It was beautiful.

Every day, I thought these children were amazing and beautiful, but to experience each and every one of them at this soul level was awe-like to me. I had stopped whispering the song and instead heard soft instrumental music playing that fed my soul and made my heart sing with joy. At that moment, I never felt more love, peace, or joy in my entire life. I knew the rest of my life would be changed forever and I was very grateful for this life changing experience. I want to tell you that the children never lost hope and neither did I; we received our miracle that day. There was no pain; there was only true love, peace and joy surrounding each and every one of us. We experienced pure unconditional love. There is no greater gift on Earth than this. The children were all smiling and my heart was pounding with joy. My heart was changed forever that day. I was blessed. Please be the love and continue this "Circle of Love" in our honor.

L's Life Message:

I have to tell you something that probably won't make sense to you at this time. It is a simple message but very powerful if you try to understand it and follow it. Here is a message to help you find your solution to stopping mass acts of violence.

You will only have an impact on stopping these types of tragedies when you start noticing the miracles right in front of you every day. It is after such tragedies that people stop; they listen and they notice the miracles. If you stop and notice the miracles each and every day, there will be no need for these tragedies to continue and they will become less and less.

The reason a murderer kills him self after this type of incident has to do with what I said in the beginning of my message. The person who takes his own life directs all of his anger, disappointments, and insecurities toward his own self. A person who takes another individual's life directs all of his anger, disappointments, and hatred towards the person that they kill or hurt. Once a murderer releases his anger towards another and kills him, he realizes that his pain is still there. He is only left with his own self-loathing. He realizes at that moment that violently directing his anger toward another individual doesn't relieve him of his own pain. In that moment of realization he takes his own life to stop the pain he was originally feeling. He wants the pain to stop so he takes his own life.

I am peaceful and happy. My death was beautiful. I did not feel any pain. I do not have any regrets. I have forgiven the shooter. He did not hurt me or take anything from me. I know you cannot understand this right now. I just need you to know that there was no pain or fear. Everything was very peaceful and I am happy and at peace. I am still with you all of the time and I like it when you celebrate the good parts of my life. Please remember, I am not suffering and I am in a happy peaceful place. I love you all and I lived my life to the fullest. My ending was beautiful! We were at peace and surrounded by pure unconditional love. I got to experience my one wish of being a mom. It felt amazing. I am at peace and surrounded in pure love, please let this message be the beginning of your healing and your forgiveness.

In God's Love, L.

CHAPTER V
Hello my name is Sharilyn

I was depressed most of my life. I was born into a very toxic life and it got progressively worse as I got older. The first time I was physically violated, I was three years old. Can you even imagine this? A three-year-old, pure, innocent toddler, who couldn't hurt anyone or defend herself, my mother always had men at our apartment trying to fulfill a deep need that she had. She used a combination of various drugs, men, and alcohol. I was just an innocent child who had no trusted adults available in her life.

I lost control at a very early age. My life continued this way for years as I further and further developed a hate for myself. I craved the attention of any man who looked my way. Most of them had the distinguishing smell of alcohol on their breath. When you have your body violated and pure innocence robbed from you, it literally seems like there is nothing that can help you to restore it. Did you know that a child has a sweet scent to them that is so pure and fresh? If they are physically violated they lose this scent and the perpetrator gains it. The child will crave and crave to get that innocence back so they will become marked. It is almost like every other violator knows this child has been exposed. The violator cannot rid himself or herself of the scent they stole from the child, but it no longer smells sweet. It is rancid and makes them crave more. It is a vicious circle that must end.

Sharilyn's Life Message:

Here is the truth that I now know. Your heart is your secret key. No one on this Earth can stop your heart from loving. You need to start with loving yourself first, no matter what the outside world deals you. Your heart is yours and it is connected directly to your soul. This seems like a ridiculous thing to say but it is actually very powerful. Using your heart to love determines who you will turn out to be. If you allow your heart to turn bitter or cold as I did, you will end up like me. I don't want to describe the graphic details of my death because it will distract you away from my message and lessons learned. Anyone can steal something physically from you, but they have no power over your heart if you decide to let it continue loving, and I don't mean in a vulnerable way, but in a pure tiny dose way. A way that is so subtle that people may not even notice right away. They will just sense something beautiful about you. Something pure, even if you believe your pureness has been stolen. No one can steal your heart.

It is kind of a funny thing to me now because it is such a simple but profound message. Think about it. Take someone who has hurt you in some way. It doesn't matter what the circumstances are. Getting your heart hurt is so painful. Only the owner of the heart knows and understands the level of the pain. If you can get one tiny seed of love and allow it to sprout, you will stay in control of your own destiny. You will become your own source of joy. You do not have to become a doormat or even direct your heart of love toward the one who hurt you. Although this would be quite powerful. It is just as powerful to direct love and positive thoughts toward a perfect stranger. That is the kind of love I am speaking about. It will bring a sparkle to your eye. A deep grounding to your soul. This is the message that I wanted to share with you.

Message from Author:

The other day I absolutely had the worst day at work. I work for someone who thrives on stealing joy and confidence from others. I refer to this type of person as an "energy stealer." Even though I have studied and practiced so many spiritual tools and even though I consider myself a very grounded individual, I still find certain situations difficult. Working for a person who steals energy is one of my challenges. Sometimes I even find it depressing. I understand what Sharilyn is speaking about.

I don't remember what happened that particular day at work. I just remember driving home and feeling completely drained and depressed. I remember having the feeling that the life had been sucked out of me. I also remember thinking I shouldn't be feeling this way. I have an amazing husband and three beautiful daughters. How can one person make you feel this bad? I had to stop to get gas on my way home. I have had my car for ten years and I always pump my own gas. When I pulled up to the pump and got out of my car I realized my tank was on the other side of the car. I got back into the car and swung around to another pump. I got out of the car and I couldn't believe it, I did the same exact thing. The pump was on the opposite side of my gas tank. I was exasperated. I got back into my car again and made a third attempt to get gas; there was only one gas pump available. It was busy at this gas station and the last two times I got out of my car to pump gas another car immediately pulled up behind me to wait their turn so when I had to move my car they moved right up to the pump. My third attempt was a success.

I got out of my car, which was now facing in the right direction. As I got out of my car, I heard a man next to me on his cell phone. He was going on and on about what a bad day he had and how he ran out of gas and he didn't know how he was going to get home because he lived two and a half hours away. He was pacing back and forth. I knew this man wasn't completely on the up and up but I also knew I had to help him.

After filling my gas tank I walked over to this man and asked him if there was anything I could do to help him. I said, "Sir, what do you need?" He started flapping his arms up in the air and pacing even faster and he started to tell me his story. I put my hand up very gently and said, "Sir, I don't need to hear your story, just tell me what you need." He stopped and looked at me as if he was surprised and then he said, "I need some gas to get home." I said, "OK then I will help you." I placed my credit card in the pump he was parked at. I looked toward the store and I saw three young male workers inside laughing. I could hear their thoughts "sucker." I didn't care. I needed to change and shift my mood before I got home to see my husband and girls and I knew the only way to do that was to do an act of kindness for a complete stranger.

I was lost in my thoughts when I heard the man ask me how much he could get. I asked him what he meant? He said, "How much gas can I get?" I said, "We are going to fill your tank." He had a complete look of shock and confusion and he asked me again, "Why are you doing this for me?" I told him I was going to ask him for something in return when we were done filling his gas tank. He asked me if it was going to get him arrested. I started to laugh, "no of course not." He looked at me very suspiciously. This made me laugh even harder. He was the one who was ranting and raving just a few minutes earlier and he is looking at me as suspicious? I continued to pump the gas. He asked me again, "Why are you doing this for me? You don't even know me." I answered him with a smile on my face, " I heard you saying that you live two and a half hours away and I don't want you killing some innocent family on the highway because you ran out of gas going sixty five miles an hour." I think this confused him even more. All I knew is that my depression and bad mood from my terrible day were both gone. Just like magic. Poof! Gone! One little tiny act of kindness. You can't beat it.

He finished filling his tank and just kept saying, "I can't believe you helped me, can I mail you a check?" I said, "No, I don't want your money." He said "then what do you want from me?" I looked back at the store and I saw three males workers with their faces pressed against the glass just looking at me. I think they were trying to hear our conversation. I asked this man what his name was. He said, "It's Greg" I said, "OK Greg here is what I need you to do; I want you to pay this forward." He asked me what I meant. I said, "Pick a random stranger within the next week and do a random act of kindness. It does not have to cost you any money, just make a conscious effort to do something kind for someone you do not know." I told him if he did this it would change his life forever. He was just staring at me trying to process what I was saying to him. The next thing I heard him say was "So, you don't want me to pay you back?" I said. "No, I want you to pay it forward and do something nice for someone else." He broke out into a huge grin and said, "OK. I can do that."

I turned and walked back to my car. Once inside I looked over at Greg. He was just standing at the pump shaking his head back and forth. I rolled down my window and said "Greg, next time you run into car trouble, pray to Archangel Michael to help you. He can help with cars/trucks." He said, "Who's that dude? Never heard of him." I got a big kick out of that. I explained who Michael was to this man. He was just standing there smiling. He jumped into his truck. When I got to a red light and looked in my rear view mirror, Greg was still shaking his head in disbelief. I went home so happy that when I walked in the door my husband said, "How was your day?" I smiled and said, "I had the best day ever." I couldn't believe these words came out of my mouth, but I honestly couldn't remember what my boss did to me that even upset me. I was just too happy! Small acts of kindness. They will change the world!

CHAPTER VI
Hello my name is Michael

I hung myself in my garage from the rafters. I had to stop the pain in my throat. I wasn't allowed to express myself. Think about that the next time someone wants to speak and you constantly cut him or her off. Just let them say what they need to say.

I was bullied in school. I didn't really tell anyone that I was being bullied, as I already knew that it wouldn't make a difference if I did tell someone. Except for my mom. If I told my mom she would have stepped in to try to stop the bullying, which would have made it ten times worse. I wish I could have learned how to fight back, but I didn't. I didn't have the confidence and I didn't respect myself. Here's something I have never told anyone before... I was raped when I was thirteen years old. I can still hear myself screaming. I can still smell that old musty smell of his basement. I became paralyzed. I couldn't move. I wanted to fight back and run. I could do this in my mind, but my body just froze.

What did I do to deserve this? Why me? That is the kind of a selfish question – like if not me then someone else? Did I wish it were someone else? No, I would never wish that on anyone. It is the most horrifying feeling in the world. You feel like you have lost complete control of every part of your being. You lose complete control of everything in your mind, body and soul. I cried for weeks afterwards, but I never told a soul. I was kind of an awkward; keep to yourself type of kid. This made it ten times worse.

It was the summer before high school started. I won't reveal the source, not even here, but it was a person who was held in the highest regard and thought to be completely trustworthy by society's definition. He kept his deception very well hidden. Did you know that when you get violated like that it leaves a stench on your body? You can smell it all the time. No matter how many times you shower or clean yourself the stench is still there. It is similar to the scent of death. I think that is how the other violators find you. They smell the stench. The average normal person can't smell it or sense it. They just think you are a quiet introverted person. You feel dirty all the time. You feel unworthy of love. You can't even believe that your own mother could love you anymore because you do not feel worthy. Instead, you feel guilty.

I just wanted to make a little cash over the summer to buy a new racing bike. I had already picked it out. It was blue with really cool wheels and a touch of fluorescent green in the trim. I pictured myself racing it around the neighborhood and skidding it into some sand to see if I could make it through the skid without falling. Now I hate sitting on a bike. It holds a different meaning for me. It is no longer fun, but a painful reminder of what happened to me that day. You have probably guessed by now that I have not crossed yet as I still speak in present tense like I am a human. No, I am not a human, not anymore. I am neither here nor there. I am too afraid. What if I am punished for what I did? I still believe it is my fault. I must have done something to deserve this. My mom always said, "If you are a good person, good things will come your way." How can I be a good person after what happened to me? I was supposed to get paid $20.00 to clean his musty old basement for two hours. I didn't even get paid.

I can still hear the screaming going off in my head overlaid by an evil cackling laugh. I could hear him saying, "Oh come on boy, no one will hear your screams down here. It is the weekend and I live here all alone. You are mine." I started to cry and he asked me if I wanted more? I had to leave my mind at that moment. The pain was so immense I thought I would die. I remember walking home afterwards and I just kept circling different paths trying to settle my head and getting my emotions in check. That was the day I stopped showing any kind of emotion to anyone. It was the day that I stopped speaking. I wasn't mute but I acted as if I was. My poor mother thought I was just going through puberty. A stage I would outgrow one day. That didn't happen. "No, mom my soul was stolen from my body." What do I do with that? I am a deeply troubled lost soul. I can't get that smell out of my mind. It haunts me.

The bully boys at school would taunt me. It actually didn't even hurt because I was already in so much pain. Their words meant nothing to me. In a weird crazy kind of way their words brought me comfort because they brought me validation of what I already heard in my own head over and over again. See, you really don't know what a person is going through. No one ever knew my true story. People don't really care about your story. They are so desperately trying to fit in themselves, no matter what they have to do to accomplish that. I don't really have a lesson to share because I have not crossed over to the other side yet. I am stuck. Just like I was stuck on Earth when I was there. The physical pain is gone but the fear and unworthiness are still very much alive in me.

I always thought that someday I would get married and have children. Even though I was young I liked the idea of having my own family someday. That all changed the day I got raped. I decided that day that I would never ever let another human being get close to me or touch me again. Not even my mom. If she tried to hug me I squirmed away from her. She blamed it on me going through puberty. I could see the pain in her eyes, but I could not let myself get close. If she hugged me I might become unglued and tell her what happened to me. That would cause her even more pain than me pulling away from her affection. I hope she doesn't recognize me in this story. I don't want to cause her any more pain than I already have. She would blame herself for trying to teach me to be responsible and earn what I wanted in life. She never ever would have put me in a dangerous situation and she would never be able to forgive herself for what happened to me that day.

Michael's Story stopped there.....

Message from Author:

I knew when Michael's story stopped it was because he had not crossed to the other side and he was looking for my help with this. This is something I did not want to write about in this book, as it is a sacred process that I am not ready to share, especially not in a book. I also knew if I tried to help Michael cross to the other side he would not go, he was not ready, so I stopped writing. I considered just putting the book away and not publishing it. I was frustrated and felt pressured, but I was not going to get into the whole crossing over process. So I did nothing for a few days.

Then I went back to work. I won't get into the details of my day but I will tell you that I had been dealing with a reoccurring bullying situation of my own at work. My situation was tied into the bully trying to get me to compromise my ethics, which I refused to do. I made a pact with God a long time ago. I promised I would never compromise my ethics to get ahead, or for any reason. I was surrounded by people who compromised their ethics every day; this made my job extremely difficult. They compromised their ethics so frequently, they weren't even aware they were doing it.

The situation I was experiencing at work was difficult because I worked for someone who manipulated everything and everyone to get the result he wanted. Everything this person did was self-serving. This person tried to get me to do what he wanted me to do every day, which would make himself look good with no regard for the overall health of the entire organization. When I had to meet with this person I could always smell a stench. It wasn't a body odor stench. It was much worse than that, it was like a stench of death. I had only smelled this stench a handful of times in my life. I can usually smell a stench on someone who is loaded with toxins like a cancer or on someone who is about to die. Over the past two months, I smelt this stench on this particular individual several times, but only if I was alone with that person.

I left work that day knowing that no matter what happened I could not compromise my integrity or ethics for this person or for anyone in this world. I was thinking about Michael's story on my way home, wondering if this is how he felt. You start to feel helpless in a situation like this, not knowing how to fight it or end it. You feel your power being stripped away every day. Then I remembered something so important and so critical that my grandmother taught me before she passed away. One day, when I was out for dinner with my grandmother, she taught me how to resolve issues with anyone or anything I was having a conflict with in my life. She said, "Just pray to your guardian angel to pray to their guardian angel to work out any disagreement or issue you may be having. The angels will resolve it and bring the answers back to you for the highest and best of all parties involved." She told me to never go directly to someone else's angel because that would be disrespectful. This was brilliant! I have done this exact thing hundreds of times since my grandmother shared it with me.

I decided on my drive home that I was going to do exactly what my grandmother had taught me to do for my work situation. I don't know why I did not think to do this earlier, but I was going to do it today.

I started calling my guardian angel by name (you don't need to know your angel's name to do this, they know who they are). I asked my guardian angel if she would go to the guardian angel of the person I worked with to resolve this on-going battle we had been having. I released the whole situation to our guardian angels for our highest and best resolution. Within one minute I felt the Holy Spirit's energy come to me and start filling me with his divine guidance and love. I felt so peaceful and happy.

I heard the Holy Spirit ask me to release this person and all of their negative attachments from me through the offering of forgiveness. I did this immediately. I just called the person's name three times and each time I said "I forgive you xxxxx (fill in the person's name) and I release you from my energy field for our highest and best." I asked the Holy Spirit to protect me during this process. By the third time, I repeated my forgiveness statement I had a vision of the person I was forgiving standing in front of me crying. He was stating over and over again, "Thank you, thank you, I have waited so long for you to forgive me. I had to keep doing things to "squeeze" you so you could get to the point of forgiving me." This person was sobbing as he stated this to me. This person is not an emotional individual in human form but I understood it was his higher self, speaking to me directly.

I heard the Holy Spirit ask me to protect myself and this other individual in a brilliant rainbow energy light form. I picture a swirling wispy soft rainbow light coming down from heaven and individually surrounding each of us and filling us both from the crown of our heads to deep below our feet into the Earth. What happened next was unbelievable to me.

I felt almost like a pop go off in my brain and my body felt so much lighter, as if I had lost 10 pounds of weight. I felt a sense of peace, calmness and joy that I had never felt before when thinking about this particular person. I felt like the situation was completely resolved. I felt lighter and happier and I knew that this person would no longer have any power over me. Once you forgive someone you release his or her power over you. You protect yourself very carefully prior to doing this so they can no longer attach their energy to you. This whole situation happened within three minutes while I was driving home from work. I couldn't even believe it myself. By the time I got home, I couldn't wait to run upstairs to tell my husband what had happened. The next week three different people came up to me to ask me if I had lost weight. I laughed to myself, "yes, the weight and burden of carrying around someone else's energy." I felt empowered and happier than I had in a very long time. I realized at that moment how important it was to forgive those who hurt us in any way.

That night I felt inspired to continue with this book. I didn't know why as I still did not want to discuss helping spirits cross to the other side, but I knew I had to write. As soon as I started typing I heard Michael say, "I am ready to tell my life lesson." I was stunned. I responded to him by asking him "how can you share your life lesson if you haven't crossed?" Michael said, "I crossed today, Maureen." I was even more surprised. I said, "Oh, did you find someone else to help you?" He said, "No, you helped me." I said "No I didn't" He said, "Yes you did." I asked him how? He said, "I have been following you all day and I watched what you did tonight, I watched you forgive your boss. You gave us the secret key." I asked him what he meant. Michael stated "Maureen, when you forgave your boss I realized that, that was the secret to me feeling worthy enough to cross to the other side. I followed your example and I forgave my violator. I always thought because of what happened to me that I wasn't worthy enough to cross to the other side, so I was stuck. When I saw you take your anger and turn it into forgiveness and compassion, I realized I had the power to do the same thing. You made it look so easy, so I tried it. As soon as I did, I felt so light and uplifted. I even forgave myself for all of the hateful things I said and did to myself, then I saw the light and I crossed so easily. Maureen, you helped thousands of souls cross today and you have taught us something so valuable that we never knew before. You taught us that forgiveness is the secret key to moving forward in our lives no matter what stage we may be in. You gave us such a powerful tool to use. Maureen, you taught us how to cross ourselves. No one has ever taught us this before. Usually when a soul gets stuck, we wait for someone like you who is willing to help us. Sometimes when we find someone like you we are still not ready to cross because we do not feel worthy. Now we understand that we are in control of our own destiny and all we have to do is forgive the person who has hurt us. Once we forgive we are free to move on and we are empowered to do this ourselves. This is new information that we never understood before."

I felt completely overwhelmed and emotional when I heard Michael's message. I started to cry. Wow! I never would have figured that out on my own. Nor would I have realized that this was the key to thousands of souls who felt stuck, to be free to move to where they belonged in pure unconditional love and peace. This day was life changing for me. So I asked Michael, "What is your life lesson you want to share?" He said, "Maureen, I just shared it. Forgiveness is the key to freedom and a happy future. Once you forgive someone you are no longer bound by his or her energy. Once you forgive them they no longer hold any power over you. This is such an important message for people to understand. This important message will change the world as people start practicing it. You do not have to wait until you are stuck, you can start using this secret key today to advance in your life and feel the pure freedom that it brings."

I was so emotional when I heard Michael speak those words. I felt pure joy and happiness. Who could guess that you could have a day so filled with anger and have it turn into a night of complete joy and peace. Michael, I cannot thank you enough for sharing this invaluable information with the world and me.

CHAPTER VII
Hello my name is Kaitlyn

I want to tell you my story. It is a sad one with a very happy ending. The thing I didn't realize when I was on Earth is that happiness is just a thought. It is really that simple. Change your thoughts and you can change your life into a happy one. Happiness is not something you acquire through material things or through another person. Happiness is locked in your own mind and you are the only one who holds the key to unlocking it. Change your thoughts and you will change your life. Just decide it and it will be. If you don't believe me, just try it for a few short moments. It does take a little practice, but it is actually quite simple. This was my happy ending. I am happy now but I took the wrong route to get here.

I am here to share my life lesson with you so you won't waste any more precious time here on Earth. I do mean precious. You have no idea how valuable each and every day is. Actually, each and every moment is valuable. You can't get it back once it is gone. Time is so valuable yet you waste it each and every day. You waste it by waiting for things to happen. Don't waste your valuable time waiting. The time is now. Here is my story...

I was 17 years old when I died. I hated my life. I found every single day difficult to get through. I was very pretty, but I didn't know it. Instead I would cut myself down every day. I had long silky brown hair and tiny freckles sprinkled around my cheekbones. I was slender and straight. I had a small boyish figure. I didn't wear makeup. I didn't want to do anything to bring attention to myself. My mind was so busy it never stopped thinking. I would say hateful things to myself every day. I was very quiet and barely ever spoke. My parents thought I had attention deficit disorder, so they put me on ADD medication, which made me feel even worse. I didn't have ADD. I had self-loathing. There is a major difference. I didn't hear people speak to me the first time they spoke because I was listening to what was going on in my own mind. Kaitlyn, Kaitlyn are you listening? Yes, but really I liked tuning people out. I think most people just talk to hear themselves talk. Besides, if I listen to them talking I couldn't hear myself think. I hated school and just went through the motions to get through it. I knew when everyone kept asking me about college and my future that I wouldn't be going to college. I would hear it every day. What college are you interested in? What will you be majoring in? Seriously, I'm seventeen. Why do I need to decide that right now? Stop asking me those questions. Why do I need to know what I want to be at seventeen? That is ridiculous. I am just a kid; give me some time to figure it out.

I just started my senior year of high school. I was kind of a loner. I had a few friends, but no one who really knew me, not on the inside. That was my power, not letting anyone know what I was thinking. I had total control over my own world. I did feel bad for my parents though. My poor parents could not figure me out. I was their only child. The harder they tried to reach me the further I pulled away. It was like a game for me. That is why when I asked them if I could get my license they were so excited. They felt like they finally had something in common with me to share. My dad would take me out driving but soon would lose his patience. I would drive too close to the side of the road; the closer I got to the trees the happier it made me. I would do it just to get a rise out of him. He would yell at me, "Kaitlyn, watch out! Didn't you see that tree?" I would smirk very slightly so he couldn't tell I was smiling. I would think in my mind, "Yeah I see the tree dad, boy do I see it. That tree is my ticket out of here, but first I need to get my license so I can make my plan alone."

My mom would take me driving and she was the total opposite of my dad. She would talk nonstop. She was thinking it was a great place to get to know me and to get closer to me since there was nowhere for me to go. I was actually a pretty good driver, but there was no way I was going to let my parents witness that. I didn't want them to figure out my plan. Eventually when I got tired of my mother's constant talking I would just swerve a little and wait for my mother's reaction. "Kaitlyn, watch out!" Then I would say, "Mom, I can't concentrate if you keep talking." This would work every time. Then we would drive in total silence for the rest of my driving lesson. I would play these games all of the time. It was amazing to me that my parents never figured it out. I figured out a long time ago that people believe what they want to believe. It is a lot easier for them to live that way. Humans are actually so easy to figure out if you observe them long enough.

I passed my license driving test the first time. Like I said, I am actually a really good driver but my parents never witnessed this. My parents were completely surprised that I passed my driving test. I overheard them discussing it. It was actually really funny. I only had my license for one week when I went to ask my parents if I could borrow the car to go get an ice cream. My dad was hesitant, but a few pretty pleases and a look to my mom got me through. My dad handed me the keys to his car. I can still remember the smell of the car. It smelled so fresh like the smell of total freedom. I had the biggest smile on my face. I was finally going to get out of this place. I had the radio blasting. I was singing that song "I'm a Bitch, I'm a Lover" at the top of my lungs. Didn't my parents know that I didn't like sweets? Why would I want to go out for an ice cream? Why? Because it was an easy ticket out. Didn't you remember? I don't like sweets. Ha! Ha! I had to drive by the ice cream parlor so there would be a witness, someone who could say they saw my dad's car driving down that street. I still remember the lights going out right while I was approaching it. I didn't care. I wasn't planning on stopping anyway. I don't even like ice cream. I like freedom and freedom was what I was going to get.

I took the beach road home. That was my plan all along. You can go really fast on the beach road at night because no one really drives down it. I knew exactly which tree to pick. I had driven by it a thousand times before. It was right after the beach road ended and curved. The trunk was so fat. That tree must have been 100 years old. I won't live to be one hundred. I'll be dead in less than five minutes. Total control, total peace. I was getting an adrenaline rush just thinking about it, which made me drive even faster. Right around the bend, a slant to the left, dead center, BAM! Wow! It feels like I am in the middle of a fireworks show. There were loud noises and lots of pain. There was a throbbing in my head that was so painful I couldn't hear myself think. Then after a few minutes I felt a sense of total peace. Wow! I had always been searching for this lightness, this emptiness, and this peace. Wow~ this is great! I mean really really great! I did it. I got out of my head and out of my body. No one will ever know what really happened. Well, not until they read this story.

That peace I felt lasted all of five minutes, and then I heard the sirens. Then I heard the crying and the screaming. Who is crying and screaming? They were complete strangers, people I had never met before, trying to help me. I heard someone say, "Hold on Baby you are going to be OK." No, I'm not. I'm not even in there. I am right here and I feel amazing. I can no longer feel any pain. "Hey, can you hear me? Can you see me? I am right here. Hey! Hey? Hello?"

More and more people started to gather around me and then the ambulance arrived. The EMT was gorgeous. He has huge grayish blue eyes and very large muscles. He cut open my shirt and I wasn't even embarrassed. He is so cute! Maybe he will like me. Then he starts trying to resuscitate me. I look right into his eyes and he has tears coming out of his beautiful long lashes. I hear him whisper, "Come on angel don't leave me." Then I feel his pain. I feel the pain of everyone around me. I feel a deep sense of loss. Why are all of these people crying? They don't even know me. Then it hits me hard. "Oh! I am dead!" They don't know I am right here. They can't see me. I look down and see my mangled body. I look so little. Wow! Was I really that small? Then I see the EMT, he is sobbing uncontrollably and rocking my broken body saying over and over again, "I am so sorry angel, I am so sorry." Why? This isn't your fault. I did this. This is my fault. Why did I do this? Why are these people crying? Stop crying! I can feel your pain. You don't even know me. Then I heard one lady say, "She looks like an angel." Me? An angel? Don't they know how terrible I am; how I don't fit in, not even with myself?

This is not going to be easy. The next several weeks I watched my life like I was watching a movie. I watched my parents suffer and on top of that I can feel their guilt for letting me go out that night. "You didn't do this, I did. It was my decision. I am sorry. I didn't know it would hurt so much to watch all of this grief. I thought I could just get out of my mind and body. I thought this would be a good solution. I didn't know so many people could care about a perfect stranger." Even the kids at school came to see me. There was one boy named Chad who was crying uncontrollably at my wake. I overheard some girls say that he liked me and he was trying to build up the courage to ask me out. Now he wouldn't get the chance. Wow Chad, I had no idea. I would have loved to go out with you. How do I get back into my body? I have a lot I still want to do. I have a lot I want to see and learn. Now I can see all the benefits of going to school.

Wow! This is a different kind of pain. I don't like the fact that no one can hear me or see me. I want to console my mom. I want to tell her what a good, gentle, and kind mom she was to me. I want my dad to hug me and hold me. I want to smell him. That scent that always makes me feel like everything is going to be OK. I want to thank that EMT with the beautiful gray/blue eyes. I want to go to the prom with Chad. I want to run and swim in the ocean. I want to go back.... WHAT DID I DO????? What was I thinking? I want a hotdog. Can you believe it? I am dead and I want a hotdog!

Well this is my story. DON'T DO IT! You can't change your mind afterwards. It doesn't work like that. You can't touch or feel or hold or smell. That is all part of being a human. Stay and wait, something miraculous is about to happen to you. Make it happen. Decide to be happy and accept yourself no matter what happens. Just decide. Touch and feel. Act alive. Smell the fresh air all around you. See the flowers. Swim in the ocean. Be alive every day. I wish I could have a hotdog. Learn from my mistake. Live every day of your life like it is your last and you will never want the last day to come.

Remember life is precious. Make each moment count! Kaitlyn

CHAPTER VIII
Hello my name is Theodore

I am just a plain old guy, nothing special really. I just existed. I fell in love once when I was much younger. I was literally swept off my feet. This girl wasn't good for me. I guess deep down inside I knew this but she was pretty sure of herself and very popular. I was really cast under her spell. I literally gave her everything I had, my heart, my soul, and even my mind. She did my thinking for me. She told me what to do, what to say, how to dress, and how to act. Really it was quite incredible that on some level I knew this was happening, but I continued to ignore any red alarms going off in my head. The sex was so incredible. I believe that is how she took over my soul. I sold my soul to the devil as they say. The more I got the more I wanted. I stopped listening to all reason, especially from my parents. This girl, literally had me captivated. It became like an addiction. I wanted her so much I would do whatever she wanted me to do and the reward was incredible. I never felt so alive – physically anyway.

What I didn't realize at the time was that this was sort of a game for her and there were lots of others that were captivated by her "spell," too.

One day I drove by her car in a sort of secluded area. A place where we often hung out. My heart was racing with excitement. As a young man something as simple as seeing her in a car could drive me into a frenzy. I was practically panting with excitement. I was addicted to her like a drug. As I slowly walked up to her car with a sensual smile on my face, I was half thinking "I'm about to get laid." The other half of me was practically losing it right then and there from my thoughts and the memories of all the other times I was in this exact same place with her. As I look towards her car, I see her legs straight up in the air. I started panting and screaming as I noticed a red football coat on top of her pumping up and down. How did I not notice the car rocking before? I was too lost in my own lustful thoughts. Then I felt the hard slap of reality. It slapped me hard across my face. I sank to the ground holding my head in my hands. My thoughts were screaming in my mind. I could hear them loud and clear, "She doesn't love you." I felt desperate. I need to be with this girl. I love her more than I love myself. As a matter of fact, I never even loved myself until I was with her and the way she made me feel. No one knows I am here. They don't see me or notice me as tears stream down my face. I want to go to her. Everything in my body and mind is screaming for her. Then I hear her say, "Please do it to me again! I need more." I need more? That is what she always said to me. She would say, "I want you, ask me to fuck you!" I would ask her and we would have the most passionate exciting sex that would leave me begging for more.

The car starts to rock again. My mind is screaming at me to run. I couldn't breathe or move, but I knew I had to leave before they saw me. I started to run to my car. The football player pops his head up and sees me. He starts to laugh his head off saying, "That twerp? Seriously, he can't do what I can do to you." It starts all over again. I can't breathe, I can't hear, my heart is pounding so loud I can hear it in my own ears. I can't feel anything. I am dead inside. I drive directly home. I can barely see the road through my tears. I am screaming at the top of my lungs, "I gave you everything! You had my heart, my mind and my soul. Now I have nothing!" Nothing but thoughts screaming in my head. Old thoughts of how I use to feel about myself. How can I look at myself? How can I recover? I am broken. I need to get this pain to stop. I hung myself before my parents got home. I only had 30 minutes; it only took me 15 minutes. Then it was silent. The pain was gone. The noise was gone. I couldn't feel anything. I gave my soul to another person. I didn't think about it or value it. I just followed her lead, like she was "God." Like she had some kind of power over me.

Theodore's Life Message:

DO NOT GIVE YOUR POWER TO ANOTHER INDIVIDUAL! DO NOT SELL YOUR SOUL! You cannot get it back. See the person for who they really are. Close your eyes and quietly listen to how you feel around this person. Feeling lust or being horny is not worth the price of throwing yourself this far out of balance. I hope the young ones are listening to me. DO NOT GIVE YOUR SOUL TO SOMEONE ELSE. It is yours and only yours. I knew in my heart I was not the only one, but I wanted to believe it so much that I convinced myself, and at what price? The price of my life. I have a younger brother. He is so grief stricken over my death that he has socially disconnected. I chose lust over my own baby brother who needed me and loved me more than the world could offer. I stripped him of his happiness. I stripped him of his fight. He will probably never enter into a relationship because of me. My value was huge but I didn't see it. It was right under my nose.

At my wake this same girl hooked up with another guy from my school right in the bathroom at the funeral home. She used her fake grief to gain some sympathy and then hooked him in to comfort her. This one didn't bother me. I learned the value of what I was supposed to learn. You cannot value another person more than you value yourself. I miss my baby brother. It is so painful to watch him struggle. It is even more painful to watch him cut himself. This is no way to live. You can't lower your standards. This story is not just about an addiction to sex. You can't love or value something or someone more than you love or value yourself. You won't survive. Don't fall into this trap. There are people in your life who are relying on you. You can't get them the messages you want to tell them after the fact, because it is too impossible to get them to hear you. If you think it is difficult to get a human being to listen to you while you are human, it is even more impossible to get them to listen to you when you are in spirit form. I am hoping to reach one person through my story. If that happens I will take it as part of my miracle, which will become part of my healing.

CHAPTER IX
Hello my name is Dustin

Most people call me Dusty. I was kind of a scrawny kid; brown hair, freckles, lanky body and I always had a runny nose. I was kind of unkempt. What most people don't know, mostly because I never let on, was that I was a very sensitive, likeable kid. It started out as a way to protect myself and then developed into a way of life. I developed a good scowl on my face. I was unkempt enough so that people would keep their distance from me. Brown was my favorite color. I had one pair of brown raggedy looking corduroys that I loved. I displayed on the outside what I was feeling on the inside.

When I was really young, around the age of five, I wanted to be loved and noticed so desperately. That wasn't going to happen in the environment I grew up in so I made myself look untouchable so people would either ignore me like I didn't exist, or be repulsed by me and leave me alone. I got so used to this pattern that I convinced myself that it was the truth. If you really want to know the truth, I was a scared, frightened and terrified little boy who didn't have a place to belong. It started from before I can even remember. I was never wanted. I was never cared for. I learned to develop a really good imagination so that when I was left alone – when the house was quiet, I could pretend to be whoever I wanted to be. Sometimes I would pretend to be a king so that I could rule the world and have some sort of control and some security over my life.

My favorite thing to do was to pretend that I was having an elaborate celebration for my birthday. The kind of party everyone wanted to be invited to. I would pretend there were lots of kids there, laughing and screaming, chasing each other around. I would imagine there was a huge sheet cake with trains on it that said "Happy Birthday Dusty!" I would always have two large pieces of birthday cake. I actually never had a piece of birthday cake in real life. I never had a birthday cake at all. That is what is so great about being a kid with a vivid imagination. You can pretend and imagine anything and really believe that it is true. I would imagine each kid brought me a beautifully wrapped gift. I would imagine myself slowly opening each gift with a huge smile on my face. Every time I had these imaginary parties, I would envision receiving a very large box that was wrapped with a huge blue bow on top. I knew in my heart it was going to be a very special gift. When I opened it I would squeal; it was a locomotive train, the kind where the wheels actually moved. It was my favorite gift. At night when I was trying to sleep I would pretend I was holding that locomotive train. These were my favorite memories of my childhood. Every time I heard a train whistle blow in real life my heart would race with joy, and a true sense of peace would come over me. Maybe even back then I knew that the train would bring me the quiet and peace that I desired.

Sometimes I would be so lost in my imaginative thoughts that I wouldn't hear the door open when my stepfather came home. He was always angry. There was nothing I could really do about that. If I was too quiet he would accuse me of doing something sneaky. If I made a noise he would lash out at me and yell at me to be quiet. I was the target for all of his anger. "A beating a day," that is what I would call it. I got really good at using my imagination during those beatings. I got so good at it that a lot of times I didn't even feel a thing. Not right away. Not until I tried to get up the next day and every part of my body would ache and hurt. When you come from the type of background that I did and you go to school unkempt with the same dirty clothes on every day, it is very easy for the teachers, the principal, the school nurse and the other students to just ignore you. They followed the same path as everyone else in my life. Just ignore him and maybe he will go away. What I really needed was just "one" human being, just "one" caring adult who could notice that I limped when I walked; or notice that I could use a warm meal or a cold drink, but mostly that I could use a warm bath and some new clean clothes that didn't have tears in them. I didn't even get called on in class. Sometimes I really did believe I was invisible.

I received someone else's anger every day. It was poured into my body and poured into my soul for years. What should a person do with that? I stored mine up. The funny thing about it is I knew it wasn't my anger and I knew I had two choices. I could become an angry person like my stepfather and release this anger onto someone else every day, or I could just take all of the days, the months of sadness and loneliness that had developed over the years, and just end my pain.
That was the decision I chose. I just wanted the pain to end. I wanted the physical pain to end, I wanted the emotional pain to end, and I wanted the deep ache in my heart to just go away. Yes, even though I wasn't clean or good to look at, I had a huge heart that was filled with pain and sorrow!

I walked beside the train tracks for over one mile. It wasn't that I was having second thoughts about my decision or that I was scared. I just kept walking, seeing if I could pretend or use my imagination like I had when I was a young boy. The truth is I couldn't. The further I walked the emptier my head felt. I could not even pretend anymore. I heard the whistle of the train. I didn't look up or change my stride. I just closed my eyes and felt the vibration of the train approaching from behind me. I knew the exact moment to jump. It was so loud. Louder than anything I had heard in my life. Then it was totally quiet, perfectly quiet and safe. It was a quiet that I had never experienced before. It was light and free – no worry or fear, just perfectly quiet; quiet and safe. It seems like a really weird thing to say after being hit by a train. My whole life felt sad and lonely and unsafe. Now it was quiet and peaceful.

After my suicide people felt bad. They were remorseful that they did not speak to me or look at me or offer me their assistance. It is funny how I was there for years and no one even noticed me. Now that I am gone they are regretting the fact that they didn't even try to get to know me. This doesn't matter to me now, but I am telling my story so that people will notice other people like me. No one deserves to be ignored and treated less than human. It doesn't take much to make an effort to reach out to someone. Just do it. Offer something, even if it is a crayon or a pencil, a cup of coffee or a smile. Ask them, "How are you today?" and look them in the eye. Just notice them. I was just an innocent child, just like you when I was born. The only difference is that I was born into an unsafe and unhealthy home. This is the only difference between you and me.

I needed your help. I needed you to reach out to me. I write this for the others out there like me. Look at them. Talk to them. Smile at them. Give to them. What is it that you have that you no longer use or need? Sometimes it is better to do this anonymously by just leaving a little note. So many nights when I was in that dark cold house I would imagine that someone kind would drop off a warm freshly made pizza on my front door step before my stepfather got home. I ate many imaginary slices of pizza. Imagine going to bed full on imaginary pizza? I did this almost every night. We all deserve to be loved and noticed and to be taken care of; especially the children, this is not for the privileged. It is a human right. Reach out and touch a life today, don't wait until it is too late!

Message from Author: At the end of this downloaded message I could hear the verse of a song playing in my head, "reach out and touch somebody's hand."

Dusty's Life Lesson:

The lesson I want to share with you is that it only takes one person to make a difference in another person's life. I only needed one person to notice me, maybe drop off a pizza one night when I was alone in a dark cold house starving. Give me some used or new clothes that you no longer have use for; smile at me or compliment me. Here's a tough one, touch me. Do you know how hard it is being in human form and never being touched outside of being beaten? I would have settled for one hug! If only one person would have stepped forward it would have given me hope, something to hold onto. I could have been a doctor that saved thousands of people's lives. The funny thing about not being noticed is that you become very smart. People forget you are there so you can just sit back and absorb all the information you want. Also, when no one ever speaks to you, it feels good to listen to one person speaking to another person. You can pretend they are holding a conversation with you; at least you can hear the words. People always assume if you are quiet you are not smart. Just the opposite is true. You listen, you observe, and you end up becoming a walking encyclopedia. My message is "Be the Hope!" Just give a little; a kind word or gesture will change this world. It is the tiniest acts of kindness that have the greatest impact on this world.

Message from Author:

I received this downloaded message from Dusty on January 8, 2014. I wrote it in a notebook with all of the other stories that I received. I haven't read this story since that date. Today is March 13, 2014. As I type Dusty's story I can't believe what I am reading in his life lesson. I didn't remember Dusty's story or his life lesson. On February 14, 2014, my husband and I decided to adopt five families in the community that we thought could use a surprise lift. We were going through some difficult times in our own lives. One of our daughters had developed an illness unexpectedly. I was experiencing a tremendous amount of stress at my job. We have an older daughter who is almost twenty who likes to give us a run for our money. I thought if we could show our gratitude by helping other local families in our community it would help us to realign and take the focus off the negative and give us something positive to pour our hearts and energy into.

We selected a small local establishment to help us with our mission. We wanted to stay anonymous so we could experience pure gratitude without receiving any recognition in return. I remember when I went into the establishment to talk to the owner about our plan; the owner asked me if we do this every year and where we got the idea. I stated that we had never done this before and the idea just popped into my head. Now I realize after typing Dusty's story today, that Dusty put the idea in my head. Thank you Dusty. Nothing shifts my energy more or brings me more happiness than doing an act of kindness for someone else.

I had been thinking about these families for the last several days. I thought about contacting the local paper to do a story on the idea of starting a community dinner sharing practice; one where families who need a little something extra could put their name on a list. Families in the community who would like to donate a meal would go in to this local establishment, pay for the meal and set up the delivery to one of the families on the list. Can you imagine, if ten percent of the community purchased one meal and had it delivered to another family? What a difference we could make in our community and imagine how beneficial it would be for our local businesses.

Thank you Dusty for your very critical life lesson and allowing me to be a part of your plan.

Believe In Your Truth

CHAPTER X
Hello my name is Samuel

I shot myself in the head. That was abrupt, I know. I was kind of an abrupt kid too! If I thought it, I said it. No filter. Didn't have good control over my emotions or thoughts either. Not a good way to live your life. I wish I could come back to Earth to redo my life. I know now how to have peace no matter what is going on around me. I could not figure this out for the life of me when I was on Earth.

One of the best ways to find and have peace is to be quiet. Just don't speak or react to anything around you. If someone is yelling at you just look at them and don't react. You can count to 25 slowly. By the time you reach 25 they will probably realize how ridiculous they sound and calm themselves down. One of the reasons people scream at each other is because they feel out of control in an area of their life and they want to release their frustrations onto someone else. I am not saying that they are consciously aware of this. It is something that happens deep inside of them. If you can learn this little secret it will change your life. Plus you will realize how powerful silence can be. I don't mean the type of silence people use to control another person. That is different. The silence I am speaking about comes from a deep inner peace and self-control. Believe me, I did not experience this at all on Earth and that is why I am so excited to share it with you now that I understand it fully. The other thing you can do is to not react to another person's negative thoughts or words. Instead of processing their actions or words internally, do this instead. Stop! Take a deep cleansing breath and listen to their words without taking them in.

Listen to them objectively. Tell yourself they are talking to their own self. How they feel about their own self. If you can practice this it will give you a different view of what is going on with them. Again you don't really have to understand it you are just making a conscious decision not to absorb their negativity into yourself. Boy, would my life have been different if I understood this information when I was alive on Earth. That's it! I am short and to the point! Thank you for letting me add in my two cents. Not too many people listened to me when I was on Earth. It feels good to know that many people will listen to this message now.

CHAPTER XI
Hello my name is Todd

I never really liked my name. I always thought it looked like Toad when writing it. What kind of name is Todd anyway? It is not an abbreviation for anything. It is just a short meaningless name. Oh well, it doesn't matter now. A lot of things don't matter that used to hold great significance to me on Earth. It is funny how much things change once you leave your humanness behind. For instance, all of those negative thoughts and words are gone. My mind racing has stopped. I see the beauty in everything, especially in the small things. I like myself now. Wow! That is a big one. I actually like myself. Something I couldn't capture on Earth.

Do you know how free you feel when you just accept and like yourself? It is an amazing feeling. Guess what? It is a simple decision. You can decide right now to just like yourself no matter what anybody else thinks of you. It really isn't that hard. Just try it for one day. Even if someone says something negative right to your face, decide in your mind... "You know what? I like myself." You can almost feel the smile well up inside of you. It is such a simple concept. Do you know how different the world would be if everyone just decided to like themselves no matter what anyone else had to say about it? Let me tell you, "Dramatically Different!" I am not kidding. For me, I was raised in a very fear based religious home. There was so much fear that I was afraid of my own shadow. On top of that, I was always being accused of doing something wrong, even when I wasn't. It was exhausting trying to keep up with what story I would come up with to defend myself against something that I never did or something that never really happened. You get to the point where you are so worn down that you don't even know what your own thoughts are anymore. Others' beliefs and thoughts just consume you. Then if you really do something to screw up, you feel doomed. That is what happened to me. I got myself into real trouble and I didn't know what to do. I mean, if I got into trouble all of the time for things I didn't do, what was going to happen now that I did do something I wasn't suppose to do? I wasn't going to stick around to find out. My fear was so intense that I couldn't even face going home. I was too afraid of the consequences. I took a quick exit out. The funny thing was, it never even entered my mind as to what the consequences of that decision would be. I was just too afraid to stick around to find out.

I watch my family grieve over me and because they are so stuck in fear-based religion they are too busy thinking I am in hell. I am not in hell. I am in pure peace and unconditional love. My family has never considered how I ended up here. They kept thinking they didn't teach me enough or as I like to say drill me enough. "No, believe me you did plenty of that, which is why I made my choice." It was too exhausting to carry on that way.

I am sure you are wondering how this story will help anyone else. Well, I hope one person who spends their days trying to shove their belief system down another person's throat, will read this and realize that it is not their job or place to do this. Everyone has the freedom and right to believe in whatever they choose and whatever feels right for them. No human being can alter that or force something different onto another person. It is just plain wrong. Let the people believe what they choose to believe. It does not affect your belief system or weaken it. If anything it makes it stronger because you can have an open discussion with no pressure of trying to force the other person to see your point of view. It is time for humans to embrace freedom at a

very high level. It is safe for this to occur and no one should try to stop
it.

Believe In Your Truth

CHAPTER XII
Hello my name is Samantha

Most people call me Sam. I actually loved life. From the time I was very young I loved being outdoors. I would come inside filthy. That is how I got my nickname Sam. My mother always said she swore I was supposed to be a boy. I was normal in every other way. I just felt like I was at home when I was outside. I needed that fresh air and sunshine. I kept my hair really long because I hated getting it cut, but I didn't really take care of it, because I was Sam. The dirtier I got outside the happier I was. I loved the smell of dirt. I swear it made my heart beat faster. I liked everything fast. That is why I started to ride a dirt bike. It was the perfect combination for me. I was in the dirt, well sort of, I was outside and I could go as fast as I wanted to. I felt totally free. It was the only time I could honestly forget about all of my problems. I even like the sound of the loud engine. It blocked out all of the other noises, especially the ones in my head. I even learned to do tricks on my bike. I was a real daredevil. I think my mom was right. I should have been a boy. Anyway, as long as I could do what I loved I was happy. I would refer to myself as "Sam the Man." It made me feel tough, and like I could accomplish anything. As tough as I was, I also loved flowers. I love the smell of them. I loved to plant them. Anything to do with dirt made me happy. I would plant all different varieties so I could be surprised when they would bloom in the spring and summer. I liked to change things up. No one ever really understood me. I was too erratic, not tamable at all. I know tamable is not a word, but I don't care. I like to make up my own words. I could have developed my own language. I was very smart in

75

school but I was bored so I didn't put too much effort into it. I just wanted to be free. Why do I have to go to school for 12 years anyway? What a waste of precious time. I had to be outside, so I skipped school a lot. Then I got suspended. That was intended as well. I hated being confined to one place for the entire day. Just let me be free. I could have been anything. I loved learning about mechanical things and how to put things together and take them apart. I could have owned my own dirt bike shop that sold dirt bikes. I could have also had a section where you could bring in your bike so I could fix it. I pretty much knew everything about dirt bikes and I could fix anything. I was impatient. I didn't want to have to go through all of the motions and effort it takes to get from childhood, then the dreaded teenage years, until you finally made it to adulthood. No, I wanted to get there now. I was always racing to get to the next thing. I never really embraced or enjoyed anything. I was moving too fast. My mom always said, "Sam slow down, take the time to smell the roses and enjoy them." My mom was right, I planted the flowers, watered them, treated them and waited for them to grow, but I never took the time to really enjoy them or appreciate the miracle of what they represented. How could something so delicate and beautiful make its way through all of that dirt? Patience.... It takes lots and lots of patience and care.

Here is my life lesson which of course I didn't get until I rushed through everything in my life, including my death.

Lesson #1: Don't rush through your life. Every day is precious and needs to be completely valued. It is done in a flash!

Lesson #2: It is the stuff you don't like to do that makes you appreciate the stuff that you do like to do. See the value in that because it is really important.

Lesson #3: Value yourself first. If you look to others for your worth you will never have any.

Lesson #4: Being respectful is important. Respect your body. Respect your mind. Respect others and the difference of opinion that they bring into your life. Respect your brain; it is quite an amazing creation. Most of all, respect your life! **It is a precious precious gift!**

Lesson #5: If you like flowers like me, plant them, watch them grow, smell them, and enjoy them. Embrace the whole process, not just a piece of it. This is what experiencing joy is all about. Being present from beginning to end.

Lesson#6: Always take time to do something you really love that is good for you. This will get you through the rough times or dry periods. Plan the next thing, but enjoy the process of the anticipation. There is a lot of value in waiting for what is right for you. Patience is a virtue. I just had to throw that line in. I couldn't help myself.

I forgot to mention that I had a great sense of humor too! Mom and Dad, I love you! To my two sisters, you are pretty, smart, kind, and gentle. Be proud of that! Even though we were complete opposites, I still love you. I am right here for you, so don't ever forget that!

Love, Sam or as you loved to call me, Sammy! XO

Believe In Your Truth

CHAPTER XIII
Hello my name is Greyson

It is good to be alive! Well, figuratively speaking anyway. I feel more alive now than I ever did on Earth. I was killed in a car crash. It was my fault. I was a reckless driver. This is not OK, but I am here to try to make it right. Maybe I can get through to one person to let them know to slow down and take care when you are driving a vehicle.

I was 24 years old. I thought I owned the world. I was always racing from place to place. I could have taken up racecar driving as a hobby or gone to the speedway to get my thrills, but instead I decided to use the real thing, which was a very bad choice. I killed another man in the process. This man left four young children and a beautiful wife behind. He was a hard-working man who was just going about his business working hard and looking forward to driving home to see his family that he missed so much. He was just returning from a four-day business trip and he was anxious to return home to his family. I am going to stop here to state directly to his family, *"I AM SORRY! I AM SORRY FOR MY IGNORANCE AND MY IMMATURITY! I AM SORRY FOR MY LACK OF UNDERSTANDING OF HOW CRITICALLY IMPORTANT EACH AND EVERY LIFE IS HERE ON EARTH!"* I know I can never ever take back my careless actions or help your family return to the "normal" you once knew, but I am working very hard here to make sure this doesn't happen to another family. That is all I can do now.

I am now friends with the man I killed. He has forgiven me. I just have to forgive myself. I watch the struggles and grief of his family and it hurts me every day. It is hard to witness the results of my careless actions after the fact. I get to feel what they feel, all of their pain and grief. You can't drink it away or convince yourself that this is something that was meant to be. It doesn't work that way. It is a direct result of my actions and I work every day now to pay restitution for it. The man I killed tells me every day that his family will be fine. His wife has recently met a firefighter that she will fall deeply in love with and he will protect and take over for his family. The children will also accept and love this man. They will have a happy future. The man who I killed hand selected this new love for his wife. His desire is that she will experience even more joy and happiness than when he was here on Earth himself. He works every day to ensure this will be.

I work every day with the drivers on the road, especially the ones that drive too fast or are impatient. I try to get in their heads to tell them to slow down. Don't pass someone just because you want to get somewhere faster. I can guarantee you once you pass them you will not get where you are going any faster.

Every time you see a fender-bender give thanks for witnessing this. It is a reminder that you need to slow down. The people involved with the fender bender were just saved from a more critical accident. Do you realize if you drive slower you will get to your destination faster? It is true! Try it and you will see what I mean. Don't rush through your life. There is too much to live for and there is no worse feeling than knowing that you helped to end someone else's life abruptly. Live your life every day enjoying and appreciating each experience and moment. In gratitude for the lessons that I have learned and the lives that I have saved, Greyson!

CHAPTER XIV
Hello my name is Isabelle

Most people who knew me called me Belle, which was fine with me. My story is different than others here. My main issue here on Earth was that I had a major fertility issue. I had a lot of pain and scar tissue on my fallopian tubes and it caused me to become seriously depressed. Ever since I could remember I wanted to become a mother. Then when I was thirteen and I started my cycle I knew something was wrong with me. I had the most excruciating pain every month. It was like someone was sticking a knife in my abdomen. I didn't even tell my mom in the beginning. I was too embarrassed. Eventually I had to tell her, as the pain was so intense sometimes I could not even go to school.

My family was the type of family that lived in fear, and if something was wrong with you they assumed that it was because you did something wrong. So you can only imagine what my mother thought I did to deserve this. How does a young thirteen year-old girl explain her innocence and something medically wrong that she simply has no knowledge about? I didn't even try. I just went along with it. Even the old fashioned doctor my mother took me to see was looking at me in an accusing way like I personally did something wrong to deserve this. What in the world could I have done wrong? I was an innocent thirteen-year-old girl and I suffered with no help for years.

As I got older, I knew I had to at least try to get some answers and help. When I was old enough, I went off by myself to find out what I could be doing differently. The answer came back that there was nothing I could do and I would never get the chance to experience motherhood, not in the true sense that I had my heart set on. Who would want to be with me if I couldn't give them their own child? I became increasingly depressed and felt even more guilt and shame about this whole situation. I had no one to talk to and I was convinced that no man would ever want to have a serious relationship with me. My mother would constantly remind me that I was barren and that I would have to let the men I dated know right away that I could not have children so they could find someone else who could give them a child of their own. I couldn't take this physical pain any longer, but worst than that I couldn't take the emotional pain which weighed on my mind every second of every day. I decided to end my life so that the pain would just end.

After I crossed over to the other side, I noticed that my mother even blamed me for my own death. She had no remorse or sympathy. I mean, I guess in a way it was my decision, but now that I am crossed I clearly understand that it was not my fault that I had scar tissue on my fallopian tubes and that is just how I was born. You cannot make a child feel guilty or ashamed about something they are born with. Parents need to realize the miracle of having a child. They need to understand that all children are gifts that should be cherished no matter what their differences are. We all have something less than perfect about us; this is a known fact that we continually deny. Don't focus on the differences as negative, focus on the miracles right in front of you before it is too late. One of my responsibilities in heaven is to care for all of the babies that are here for various reasons. Of course I secretly cherish the ones that were not wanted on Earth. I would have wanted any child while I was on Earth. Now I get to help with so many beautiful children and every day of my life is bliss. I now understand that my mom is a very unhappy woman who does not love herself and did not know how to love a child. "I forgive you mom. It is not your fault. Someday when you come to meet me again I will be waiting with open arms ready to receive you with unconditional love."

The main thing about the way I was raised was that I was so full of love. I had more than enough love inside myself to share with everyone. I believe when you are raised a certain way, you have an opportunity to turn that situation around, to guide your future to the way that you want your life to be. I didn't understand that on Earth, but I understand it clearly now. Every day my life is full of happiness and love. I feel rich. I would have met a great man if I stayed. Someone who would have fallen in love with me and figured out the family part with me. I wasn't patient enough to wait. I was too brainwashed to believe I wasn't worthy of love. We are all worthy of love. Every single one of us, no mater what hand we are dealt. Don't give up on yourself. That is the big key. If you stick it through for yourself no matter what anyone else says or does, the reward will be huge. Remember that please!

In gratitude for the understanding of pure, true, unconditional love, Belle.

Believe In Your Truth

CHAPTER XV
The Author's experience of Alex's Story

Today was an emotional day for me. It is not always easy being an intuitive person. I had a flash back memory of the day my sister's nephew died. His name is Alex. He was a vibrant beautiful healthy seventeen year-old boy. Alex was so full of life and so full of mischief, but most of all Alex was full of love. He had eyes so bright they sparkled. He had a smile so warm it could melt a snowman on a cold winter day. Alex was and remains to be one of the most special individuals I have ever encountered in my life.

I remember the phone ringing late at night. I was already in bed and just drifting off to sleep. I felt a sense of urgency and I bolted down the stairs to answer the phone. I heard my sister's voice on the other end of the line. She sounded so quiet. I felt something was wrong before she could even tell me. She was away in Hawaii celebrating her 25th wedding anniversary with my brother in law. I was acting as guardian to their children while they were away. The last thing my sister said to me before she left on her trip was "Moe, if anything happens while I am away will you please take care of it." I remember getting a chill down my spine when she said this to me, but I told her not to worry about anything because nothing was going to happen.

My sister's voice on the other end of the phone sounded so small and quiet. I heard her voice cracking and I knew something was wrong. I heard her say, "Moe, it's Alex, my nephew, he was rushed to the hospital tonight and they are doing emergency brain surgery right now." It was close to midnight. I was trying to process what she was telling me. Then I asked her, "What can I do to help?" She asked me if I would pray and send Reiki to Alex. I told her I would.

I had recently worked at the exact hospital he was in, volunteering to do Reiki for two ICU patients. One person had a miraculous recovery and lived on with no sign he was ever on his deathbed. The other person who also had a brain issue, died. This devastated me even though I had never met this individual. I have a complete understanding that I am not the healer and that I have no control over the outcome. That is between the person and God but it still hurts me when they die.

At this moment, all I could think about was that I wanted to help Alex in any way that I could. I spent the next hour sitting in my great room praying and sending Reiki to Alex. Usually when I do this work, I can easily turn it over to God. This time, I was having a hard time separating my feelings. I started begging and pleading with God and the angels. I asked them to please help Alex and to heal him. I was very emotional about it. I felt so spiritually connected to Alex; I was desperate to help him and his family. I continued to send Reiki to Alex and his family the next day. It was so painful for me.

Alex was the exact age as my godson who is Alex's first cousin. My godson is like a son to me. My mind kept wandering and I couldn't stop thinking about how I would feel if this was my godson. I knew I wouldn't survive if something happened to him. My mind was playing tricks on me. The grief was consuming me. You believe you are secure in your faith, but it is so easy to get tripped up when something unexpected happens.

The next day my sister called me again. She said things were worse and she asked me if I would go to the hospital to do Reiki on Alex.

Honestly, there is no difference between hands on Reiki and distance Reiki. Alex was in the ICU and I was familiar with the process. The family would have to grant me permission to come to the ICU. I didn't know if Alex's family would even be open to me coming to the hospital to do Reiki on him. I told my sister I would only go to the hospital if Alex's parents granted me permission to come. I wanted to be respectful of his family's beliefs and I wanted to be respectful of their privacy in this critical care situation. The pain I felt in my heart was crushing to me.

The last time I saw Alex he was four years old. I didn't know him well at all but I had learned a long time ago your personal relationship with someone has nothing to do with situations like this. It is such an honor to be called to send Reiki or just to pray for someone. You become spiritually connected with the person at a soul-to-soul level. It is a complete honor and blessing when someone trusts you to help them in their worst time of need. The family asked me to come to the hospital. I was excited and scared all at the same time.

I went into my great room to meditate and prepare myself for going to the hospital. As an intuitive person you don't always know when messages will come. As I was praying and meditating I saw an angel appear right in front of me. This is a rare occurrence for me. I don't know why, but I asked him who he was. He stated his name was Metatron. I was surprised, as I had never heard of Metatron before. I was overwhelmed by what was happening. Then I heard my brother in-law's mother speak to me. It was Alex's grandmother, who had crossed a few years earlier. I heard her say, "Hi, it's Elizabeth." I asked her who she was. She said, "It's me Betty, Alex's grandmother." I got chills up and down my spine, but then I got excited. I knew she had come to help Alex with his recovery. I asked her to please help to heal Alex. I explained that he was too young and that he needed to stay here. She smiled at me warmly and said that she was here to help Alex with his transition. I asked her "what transition?" She explained that it was his time to go and that she was here to greet him. I was very scared and emotional. I had never experienced this before and it shocked me. I started begging and pleading with her to please let him stay. She just smiled at me and said, "It is his time. Everything will be OK." I remember just sobbing and crying. I felt helpless and scared. It was extremely painful knowing that something was about to occur and there was nothing that I could do to help. I wanted to desperately change the outcome.

I turned back to Angel Metatron and asked him if he could please intercede on Alex's behalf. He smiled at me peacefully and then I heard him say he helps humans with their transition to the afterlife. This unraveled me. This couldn't be happening. I was so overwhelmed. What was I suppose to do with this information? Then I decided I would work even harder. I started sending more Reiki and praying harder than I had ever prayed before in my life. I could feel my energy draining and I was getting a bad migraine, but I refused to stop. I think this is the day I realized that you cannot override a person's free will or a transition plan. It is not possible. No amount of wishing or praying was going to change this outcome.

My human thoughts kicked in, "What if I go to the hospital to do Reiki on Alex and he dies while I am in the room with him and they think I killed him?" I started to panic. I prayed that the family would change their mind and not have me to come to the hospital. At least if I didn't go to the hospital they wouldn't think that I killed him. I started convincing myself that I just imagined the whole thing, almost like a dream while you are awake and that I never heard from Betty or Angel Metatron.

I called the hospital to speak to Alex's mother and tell her I was on my way to the hospital. I was still in my driveway and I had done an excellent job of convincing myself that nothing had happened. I did not receive any further messages from Betty or Angel Metatron. I was thinking, "It was just in my mind." I could hear the phone ringing as I waited for Alex's mom to answer. I kept telling myself "Everything will be OK. He is a young healthy boy who has his whole life ahead of him." I heard Alex's mom say hello. I told her I was on my way to the hospital. She said, "No! No! Don' t come." I was surprised. I asked her, "Did you change your mind about the Reiki?" She said, "No, I didn't change my mind but the doctors just left and Alex isn't going to make it." I heard a loud thumping in my ears and I started sobbing uncontrollably on the phone saying over and over again "I am so sorry." Then I said, "Please let me come, I will do anything I can to help Alex." Alex's mom stayed calm and said, "No, Alex is brain dead and we have to decide when to pull the plug, but Alex is going to donate his organs. There is nothing you can do." I told her again how sorry I was and hung up the phone. To this day I feel bad that she had to console me in her most critical time of need.

All of the messages that I received just a few hours earlier from Betty and Angel Metatron came flooding back into my mind. How could this be happening and why did they have to tell me this information ahead of time? What good does this knowledge do if I cannot help to change the outcome? I was mad at myself for not going up to the hospital earlier. Then I heard my sister's voice in my head, repeating her words to me just before she left for her trip to Hawaii, " Moe, promise me that if anything happens while I am away you will take care of it." I knew I had to take my niece and nephews up to the hospital to say goodbye to their seventeen- year old cousin. I dialed Alex's mom again, and asked if I could bring my sister's children up to say good-bye to their cousin. She said, "Yes, Alex would love that!"

I drove over to my sister's house and I can honestly say that nothing in my life has been as difficult as what transpired over the next several hours. My most painful memory was seeing the look of devastation in my sweet nephew's beautiful chocolate brown eyes, when I told him I had to take him up to the hospital to say goodbye to his cousin Alex. He threw himself in my arms and sobbed uncontrollably as his body shook. To this day I cannot speak about what happened that day without sobbing and reliving the pain of that memory.

We drove to the hospital in total silence. When we arrived at the ICU, the waiting room was consumed with grief. There were crying and devastated teenagers everywhere, trying to console each other. I stood by the elevator doors and just started sending Reiki into the waiting room for anyone who wanted or needed it.

My niece and nephews went down the hall to go say goodbye to their cousin. I felt completely helpless in this situation. I prayed and sent positive thoughts. I did anything I could think of, just hoping that I could bring some solace to someone, anyone, as a hope that it would help and at the same time make me feel better. It didn't! There are no words, gifts, food or drink; there is nothing you can offer that will take away the pain. I even had questions about my own faith and strength! The only thing I had to offer was a warm smile, a gentle hug or a kind word. It felt so insignificant.

When my niece and nephews came back down the hallway they looked so helpless. My niece appeared to be holding up the best. She was fifteen years old and the youngest. We walked over to say hello to their uncle. He looked at me and said, "Hey Moe, can you take the boys to get new suits tomorrow? They are going to be pallbearers." This is when it hit me the hardest. My nephews looked crushed. Just hearing those words made everything so real. My niece reacted for the first time and looked shocked. I thought I was going to fall over. His words left a stinging pain in my ears. My heart was crushed, pallbearers for their precious seventeen-year old cousin? Why? They were seventeen and twenty years old. Why at their young ages would they have to face this devastating situation? I told their uncle I would take them the next morning. I was so happy to be able to do something to help.

We left the hospital and drove home in complete silence. The boys asked me to drive them home so they could have some time alone. My niece wanted to come back to my house with me. About an hour after we arrived at my house, I was sitting on the couch beside my niece. Her voice was so quiet that at first I didn't even realize she said something. Then I heard her say, "I didn't know, Auntie!" I asked her what she said. She repeated in the same soft voice, "I didn't know auntie!" I asked her what she meant. She said, "I didn't know, Alex was going to die. I didn't know we were going up to the hospital to say goodbye to him." I held her for the longest time as she grieved over the loss of her cousin. It was another devastating blow. She had stayed at another cousin's the night before and she wasn't home when I had told her brothers about Alex. I did such a terrible job in telling them as I was sobbing more than they were that I knew when she arrived, I couldn't deliver the message again. I asked my nephew if he could tell her. He said he would. I found out later he just told her they were going up to the hospital to see Alex. She already knew Alex was in the hospital. She had no idea that when we went up to the hospital it would be her last time to see her cousin. That is why she was doing so well. She only understood that Alex was going to die when she heard her uncle tell me to take the boys to get new suits so they could be pallbearers.

The next day I took the three of them funeral shopping. It was Mother's Day. I decided that I had to bring some joy into this day. For the entire car ride we talked about the funniest movies we ever saw and I made them imitate the funniest lines. We were laughing so hard on the way to the store that it actually felt like a normal day for a little while. While we were shopping the boys really got into shopping for their suits and at one point they were arguing over one particular suit jacket that they both loved and wanted. We found our joy that day, even if it was only for a few short hours.

The funeral was one of the saddest that I have ever been to in my life. I looked over to my left and I saw Betty there all dressed up in a pretty soft periwinkle dress with a nice matching hat. She looked amazing! Her blue eyes were beautiful and nearly matched the color of her dress. She smiled at me and reminded me that everything was going to be OK. She looked so beautiful and healthy! I blinked my eyes, which is what I always do when these things happen and when I opened them again she was gone. I did hear her say, " I will take good care of him!" She had the biggest smile on her face.

I remember the first line of the eulogy, "Do you believe in angels? Because I do!" I started to cry. I remembered the angel that came to visit me in my great room to tell me he was coming to help Alex with his transition to the afterlife. It brought back all the pain of knowing there was nothing I could do to help or stop this outcome. It is such a helpless feeling. I asked Alex telepathically, "Hey Alex, will you be communicating with me?" Instantaneously I heard him say, "What do you mean? I already have! You just need to listen to me." This brought even more tears. Yes, he had been communicating with me. Alex was perfectly accepting of his death. He had no regrets and he went willingly. It hurts me to even write this. It is not the person crossing who has the issue or suffers. It is the one who stays! It is the one who loses the loved one that has the most difficulty.

Alex was happy with his life here and very excited about returning to the life he knew before coming here. His grandparents and his great grandparents greeted him peacefully! Alex is peaceful and happy!

Alex made the decision to donate his organs on the day he was rushed to the hospital. He stated earlier that day that he couldn't imagine anything better than being healthy enough to help others by donating his organs. Alex did exactly that. He saved six people's lives.

May 5, 2014 - Alex's Life Message:

Hello my name is Alex,

I am very much alive. As a matter of fact, I am more alive now than I have ever been. I love my life. I was always kind of full of life but sometimes I took things too far. I guess that is understandable based on my age. I don't want you to grieve over me any longer. I know my anniversary is coming up this weekend. But I am happy and alive. I have not left you. I am with you all the time.

To my family members, please make better choices for yourself. Grieving will not help you and it will not bring us closer any sooner. You need to focus on making good and positive choices. Bring joy to someone else every day. That is a secret ingredient. I think I was good at doing that while I was on Earth.

My message to the people who never knew me on Earth, "Embrace and treasure every moment of your life. A lot of you are walking around completely depressed waiting for something to happen. Don't! You make it happen. When you are ten years older than you are right now, you will say things to yourself like, "Oh! I will! When I was xxxx I wish I did more of... or I wish I took that leap of faith!" OK, then do you want to say that again after another decade? The answer is "No!" By the way, I was only seventeen when I died. I had no idea what I wanted to do with the rest of my life. I was positive about one thing though; I wanted to make a difference in someone else's life! I actually made that decision on the day that I was rushed to the hospital. Actually, it was only a few small hours after I made that decision that I collapsed. I did not take my own life. I was born with something that no one was aware of. It was in the cards as they say. I am OK with this. I did exactly what I came to do. I did not exit before my time. It was exactly as planned. I am peaceful with everything.

I will state here for anyone who is considering rushing their plans along. Don't do it! You are not meant to take your own life. You are meant to serve a promise and commitment that you chose. No matter what happens in your life, especially the unplanned shocking stuff (like my death) you must remain true to your mission.

Make things happen. Never ever rely on another human being to make things happen for you. Not your spouse, your parents, your siblings, definitely not your boss or friend. If you do this, you will be unhappy for many more days or years until you read this again and realize that you had the missing ingredient the whole time. You get to decide and make your own choices. It is just a decision as they say. Decide it and take small steps toward it every day. Celebrate your little successes by rewarding yourself and keep yourself moving in the right direction. You will have a happier, more peaceful life if you can do this.

For what it is worth, I just want you to know that if I were dealt a different hand, I would have stayed to be a teacher and a coach. I would have wanted to work with all of the unruly high school kids. Why? Because I was one of them and I get how they think and why they do the things that they do. I would have been a great teacher, so I am taking this opportunity to teach you right now. I am teaching you what it is that I have learned. I was full of love on Earth and I am full of love here. Make the decision right now to turn your life around and be happy. You will be grateful that you did.

A special message to certain loved ones (you know who you are). Stop the destructive behaviors right now! Honor me by carrying on and making me proud. I am proud of you and I love you. By the way, I hear you speaking to me and I try to communicate back to you but honestly you SUCK at listening. See I just heard you say, "What?" Give it up, just start listening. I have to listen to your whining and woe is me stuff every day. Also, your way isn't working so why don't you try it my way. You know I always had the better ideas. I love you all, each and every one of you, even those that I did not physically get a chance to meet on Earth.

P.S. Have fun at my anniversary tournament. I am there every year. See if you can sense me or smell me this year.

You are the best! Please know that we celebrate birthdays in heaven. So when you are celebrating my anniversary of death, I am celebrating my birthday in heaven. Won't you join me in celebrating my heaven birthday by having a birthday cake for me on that day and singing "Happy Birthday?" This in itself will help you to heal.

 All my love... Alex

P.P.S. I am a better person because I got to experience you in my life! Now pass that on to others and stop wasting time! xo

Believe In Your Truth

CHAPTER XVI
Hello my name is Andrew

I like to be called Andrew, although some people liked to call me Drew. I didn't like it and I got tired of correcting them, but I would still cringe when I heard them say it. When I was really young a few mean kids would call me Drool and I really hated that. I was a quiet kid but I expressed myself through my love of sports. Off the field you wouldn't get much out of me but on field I came alive. I played everything from baseball to football. I loved them all but football was my favorite. In hindsight, I think I understand why a lot more now than I did while I was on Earth. Football is a grueling sport. You wouldn't really understand that unless you ever experienced playing it. My coaches throughout the years were brutal. I think it helped me in a way because I had so many negative thoughts going through my mind about myself every day that when they said negative things to me it felt like a good release. The rest I could work out through beating my body to the ground. This is not a healthy choice. You do not get rid of your self-loathing through someone else saying you are good for nothing and that you are never going to amount to anything. It feels good at the moment to release your own internal pain and to hear someone say what you tell yourself every day, but really it just builds up more negativity, layer on top of layer.

Now, I find it is so interesting that many people look at someone like me, (I had great success in sports; I was a good looking guy and the fact that I was quiet made the girls even more attracted to me) and they see what they want to see. They never really see what is going on inside of a person or what is happening in their mind. That was my problem. I had a lot of negative stuff going on in my mind and body that no one could see. I would work my muscles to the bone trying to get these negative thoughts to stop, but I couldn't. This sounds depressing to me as I am saying it. So, if I don't tell you what I have learned, my story will be pointless. I learned that thoughts are just that.... thoughts. You can decide at any moment to change them. This is an easy process. You may have to pretend in the beginning, but the key is to start saying positive things to yourself every day. Even if you don't believe them, you have to do it. It also helps to write them down and read them to yourself every day. If you are afraid to do that for fear that someone else will see them, type them into your electronic notes on your smart phone. Writing them is important. If you are brave, post them on your bathroom mirror so you can start your day on the right foot and end it the same way.

Here's my other message, "*WHO CARES!*" Something that I have learned since my crossing that I didn't understand beforehand is that the people who are criticizing you... the teachers, the coaches, the priest, your friends, your enemies, etc., they are doing so because they are saying the things to you that they believe about themselves. Please don't miss this point, it is important. I am going to repeat this message again; the people who are criticizing you are doing so because that is how they feel about themselves. If you can get this one message then I have done my job here. Once you understand this then you can apply a different method when someone says or does something negative to you. You can say something to yourself in your own mind like, "I know you are, but what am (with a little smirk on your face); or Oh! I am sorry you feel that way about yourself." Believe me, just making this small change will start to change your life. You will view people from a different light and you won't be so serious. I wish I knew this when I was on Earth. It would have made things so much easier for me. When I go back through my life review and I apply this lesson, I see my entire life in a totally different view. Wow! I could have done so much more with my life if I applied this one principle. If I help just one person I will be happy, but secretly I am hoping to help the masses.

In good health and light! Andrew.

Believe In Your Truth

CHAPTER XVII
Hello my name is Stephen

I am shy about telling my story. First let me just start with saying I never would have spoken to or believed in a medium while I was on Earth. I didn't believe in any of that stuff. Now of course, I want my story to be told, and this is the only avenue I have to work with. It still blows my mind that you can hear me, because most people can't. They didn't really hear me while I was there on Earth either. Did you ever really notice that people just don't listen? Most of the time when you are speaking to them they are so busy trying to figure out what they want to say that they will politely or not so politely wait for you to take a breath or a sigh, and then they will jump right in to tell their story. Humans have very busy minds, so when you talk to them most of the time they are thinking about what they want to say back to you, hence, why they make terrible listeners.

Did you know listening is the quickest way to learn? That is why little babies get smart so fast. They listen all of the time. They are like little sponges just waiting for the next bit of information you will share with them. When I was a baby, I was so curious. I would listen to everything. I didn't talk too much but I would take it all in. Even by the age of three I wasn't talking too much. I understood everything and probably knew more than most adults. I was locked in my own mind. Talk about a busy mind. It is like you are trapped in your own brain. You know what you want to say, but you can't formulate the words to get the information out. If you think it is frustrating trying to get someone to listen to you in your life now, try getting someone to listen to you when it takes you forever to formulate a sentence or an idea. They will bypass right over you like you don't even exist and make you feel like you don't even matter. It is painful. Just because a person can't explain themselves like a normal person would, doesn't mean they can't feel all of the same pain and disappointments. My life was full of disappointments. People think because you don't talk that you are stupid. No, contrary to this belief, people like me understand more than most human beings do. That is why I think it is so cool that you can hear me. You are listening to me telepathically right now and you are having a hard time typing as fast as I am speaking. Now, if someone could only figure out how human beings can speak and be listened to telepathically, it would be really amazing for someone like me. My suffering would have stopped. I would have felt valued and appreciated.

Do you know what it is like to be in a school meeting, sitting there and having people talk about you like you are not even in the room? Then they say things like "Oh! You poor thing." Seriously, I can hear you; I am not deaf or stupid for that matter. Bored? Yes, I am bored. I could teach the class better than you do because I have watched more T.V. and listened to more conversations. I loved the discovery channel. I have read more books. Yes, I can actually read. You thought I was only looking at the picture because I would turn the pages so quickly. No, I read those pages, every single one of them. Plus, because I don't speak, adults would speak right in front of me all of the time and forget I was there. I knew who was having an affair, who had lost his job, who gained or lost weight, what was on sale at the grocery store, and who won the ballgame. Amazing, all of the different conversations that can come up. Thank God for all of these conversations, otherwise I would have gone stir crazy. It is lonely to be ignored day in and day out. By the way, saying, "You OK, buddy?" does not qualify as conversation.

I used to think about the fact that if I could just form my words and speak them, how many people would be shocked at how much I knew. I even knew about the stock market and how to make lots of money. No one ever listened to me or asked me anything with the exception of, "Are you OK, buddy?"

"Yeah! Yeah! I am OK! Are you OK? Cause your husband is cheating on you!" How's that for a shocker? Obviously, I still have a little anger about how I was treated. I am currently working on forgiveness. Just because you are no longer in human form doesn't always make things like forgiveness easier. I already decided if I come back to Earth again, I am going to be a counselor, because that way I can get paid at something I am really good at... listening. Then when I do talk people will listen because they will want me to try to solve their problems.

So, what could I have done in this lifetime better? Well I could have smiled more and let my emotions show a little more. Then people would have understood that I was processing everything that they were discussing. I also could have removed myself from the situation when the situation was too painful. Instead, I chose to just sit there looking lifeless. I don't really blame the people who were observing me. What were they suppose to think. I would have spent more time at the beach, too! That was one word I could say. I used to practice it at night when I was alone in my room. It is only one syllable so it wasn't hard for me to formulate. I loved everything about the beach. I loved the wind and the sand, the sun and the water. I actually felt real at the beach because at the beach, people don't do a lot of talking. They just lay around relaxing or they read a good book or magazine. I blended right in with them. I look pretty normal, so no one would know I was different. The other reason I loved the beach had to do with sensory touch. It was actually painful for me to have my skin touched. It was like having raw nerves. After pulling away for so many years, people including my own family just gave up trying to touch me. Even light touch bothered me. When I was at the beach, in that warm ocean water it was like I died and went to heaven. It felt so good to me. I would sit in that water for hours. Those were always the nights that I slept the best. It was the high concentration of salt that was so soothing to me. It would help to sooth me in so many ways.

Stephen's Life Lesson:

My life lesson isn't a huge one. It is just one small piece of information that could help hundreds and hundreds of people, if you would just "listen" and follow it. Telepathic communication is just as powerful as speaking. I would argue that it is even more powerful than speaking. Next time you see someone who you would consider disabled in any capacity, look them straight in their eyes and warmly smile at them. You don't even need to say hello. If you are going to speak to them do so telepathically. Then really focus and listen to their response. I think you will be very surprised at what you hear. I think if only 10 people get this message and start to implement it, we could have a more peaceful world in the near future. Like I said, it is not a huge life lesson, but it is an important one. I hope you will reflect on it and try it for one week. See what you notice and how different that person looks after they hear you speak to them telepathically.

Maureen, you changed my life! Thank you for listening. From a place of complete peace and happiness, Stephen.

CHAPTER XVIII
Hello my name is James

My story is a little different than everyone else's story here; I led a very non-traditional life on Earth. First, let's just start by saying I was not always a nice guy. As a matter of fact, I think most people who knew me may say I was a little off my rocker and definitely a little intimidating. I did a lot of things that I am not proud of. When I was on Earth I didn't filter. I didn't distinguish good vs. bad or right vs. wrong. I just did whatever I felt like doing whenever I felt like doing it, with no thought or remorse. This is where the problem laid. If you don't have a filter and you don't care about what the results of your actions are, you continue to make one poor decision after another. Then the lies start. You lie to cover up the first act and then so on and so on. You get to a point that you don't even really know what the truth is anymore. The funny thing is, it is so easy to lie. So many people just believe what you tell them. I agree with the last guy, Stephen. If you practiced communicating telepathically, then you would be able to easily figure out when someone was feeding you a line of bull. People were so intimidated by me that they just believed whatever I told them. This started when I was much younger. If I wanted something and I didn't have the means to get it the right way then I went to Plan B and used my bullying tactics to get what I wanted. Once I got a reputation, people would just give into me right away. After that, you find a few loyal people in your life that believe you no matter what. They will stick up for you to the bitter end. Even if deep in their mind and heart they know it is not true, they will convince themselves otherwise. This is not good, as it leads to a pattern of destruction, which continues to get stronger.

Here is something I didn't know when I was there on Earth. All of your actions, no matter what form they take (your thoughts, your words, your hands or your weapons), end up with you being accountable for them. Even if you think you get away with something, you really don't. Even if you believe no one saw what you did or heard what you said, someone somewhere does and it matters. You may not understand this at the time of your thoughts or actions, but believe me you will someday.

In my specific case, my family members are the ones who continue to suffer because of all of my ignorance and lack of empathy. They will never be the same. I put them through hell and the residual effects continue to linger even today. How do you explain to your friends or girlfriend that your dad had a hand in killing and destroying others? How do you explain that your dad was in prison? How do you explain that your dad did terrible things his whole life and then he took his own life in the end? It is one failure after another. My family has to live with my poor decisions and actions every single day for the rest of their lives. Every time I can't be at one of my boy's games to cheer them on, my pain continues. Every time I have to watch my wife continue to struggle financially it is a reminder of what I created. I was bitter and mean. I didn't care about anyone but myself. I would pretend I did, but I didn't. It was all about me. The funny thing is, the more I cared about myself, the less happy I became. That is what continued my pattern of self-destruction. You get a rush of adrenaline from your chosen actions. That feels good until you crash. You can't deal with the let down, so you look for the next rush of adrenaline. It is a vicious, and deadly cycle. I am no longer proud of my destructive behavior. I can see now how much more I could have done with my life. I can see how much time and energy I wasted on destroying other people's lives; this includes my own family.

My main issue was anger. I had so much of it that I didn't know what to do with it. It would fill me up and I had to release it. I could have released it in a healthy way by giving my all to sports or running or helping someone else, but I didn't. Instead I did something to release my anger only to realize that it was still there and even stronger the next day. I am going to move into my life lesson because this is beginning to depress me.

James Life Lesson:

The life lesson I have learned since I crossed over to the other side is that I was just a sweet, sensitive kid who was actually very shy and easily embarrassed. I absorbed a lot of fear, anger, and criticism from the adults around me. I didn't know how to filter this anger, so as I internalized it, I kept storing it up. Sometimes at night, I would punch my pillow trying to release this pain. That actually didn't work. As I moved into my teenage years, I realized that if I were mean to someone else, it would actually release some of my own pain. This is how my destructive pattern started.

My life lesson was to learn that if you treat other people with kindness and you do something nice for them you "can" release your pain a lot quicker. It is actually that simple. Just doing something nice for someone or reaching out to another kid who is struggling will make you feel a lot better about yourself immediately. I don't know if I ever would have figured this out while I was on Earth. I was too wrapped into my cycle of anger and destruction. I was too insecure. It is amazing to me how simple the answers are once you quiet down all of the outside clutter. If you have an anger management issue, or a self-hatred destruction issue try to do small acts of kindness for someone else and watch how you can easily transform your life. Otherwise you will watch all of the people you truly love and care about suffer because of your decisions and actions.

Just make a choice, but be sure it is a good one. The effects will last a lifetime. J

P.S. I want you to know that I spend all of my time now interceding to save other people's lives. It is the most rewarding and fulfilling thing I have ever experienced. My insecurity is completely gone and my heart is filled with more unconditional love than I know what to do with. I am the big mushy marshmallow type now and I am proud of it. I am free of all my internal pain and unhappiness. If I had stayed I would have ended up with Parkinson's disease and been even angrier than I was before. I am better off here so I can make a difference in as many people's lives as I can without being a burden or embarrassment to anyone else. I am happy, I am free, and I am alive.

I ask that you please forgive me for all that I have done to cause you pain. I know that is a tall order, but it will help me to help even more people if you can grant me this gift. I send you my love. It is only in giving forgiveness to another that you can experience pure bliss and joy there on Earth. Try it and you will see what I mean. It is not worth the price of holding onto your pain. It will destroy you or someone else. Let it go and set yourself free! In peace!

CHAPTER XIX
Hello my name is Jay

I was a bully, too! I hate to admit that now. I am ashamed of my behavior. I was able to turn the corner before it was too late. I went to a technical high school and fell in love with learning every aspect of auto mechanics. It saved my life. It is actually funny to hear myself say that. What I mean is, I got so engrossed with fixing automobiles that I ate, slept, and breathed them. This passion kept me out of trouble and helped me to focus on other things.

I started following antique car shows. I actually built my own business fixing and replacing parts on old antique cars. At first, I just went to the shows because I loved cars so much. Then I started socializing with the owners of the cars. Then I got involved with their conversations about their cars. Next thing I knew, I was fixing their cars and replacing the old parts. I got to open my own specialty shop at the age of twenty-five. It was my passion and my love. Then one day it all came crashing to an end. I was twenty-seven years old. I had the world by storm. I loved getting up every day and going to work. Every time I fixed another specialty car it was like fixing a piece of my soul. I was in heaven. Then one day I was under one of those precious cars and the car slipped off the ramp. It was before your modern technology today. As a matter of fact, my death led to some of the technology changes that you have the convenience of having now. It is rather ironic, since I love cars more than life itself, and the car actually crushed my heart. It was quick and my pain only lasted a few minutes before the sense of peace came over me and I felt lighter than I ever had in my life. Today, I enjoy my life every day. My specialty is trying to help the youth choose a career that they love.

Jay's Life Lesson:

My life lesson is one that I already got to experience before my crossing. Most people don't figure out their life lesson until after their life on Earth is complete. Here is my life lesson. Live your life every day doing what you love. Don't follow the patterns and processes of everyone before you. You have to get in touch with what makes you tick inside. I feel so bad for these kids today who are so pressured to answer to the questions, what do you want to do or be? How do they know? They have to be exposed to different things from a young age so they know what they like and what they don't like. As a society we need to demand that our youth experience more hands on learning instead of sitting in a hard wooden chairs for six to seven hours a day. This is so unhealthy and it doesn't help to stimulate the brain and emotions. The only reason I found out what I loved was because I went to a school that exposed me to hands on experience and learning. Then I pursued the rest on my own by doing what I loved, the rest just kind of fell into place.

Listen, find out what makes you tick inside and focus on that. Anything less than that will just make you old, sick, and depressed.

This is my message for you. Follow your heart! Jay

P.S. My mom always used to say I was short and sweet and to the point. I guess my story validates that too!

CHAPTER XX
Hello my name is Lou

Honestly, I didn't think I would come through in this book. I am still shocked that I ended my own life. I was one of the kids that Jay is speaking about. I followed the "perfect" pattern. I followed all of the rules. I did all of the right things according to the plan that was laid out for me. I was an all sport star in high school and that continued into college. I was a gifted student as well. I was good looking and I came from a really really good and loving family. So why did I make the decision that I made? Because I felt completely empty inside. I could not feel anything. That is what happens to a person that follows the plan that is laid out for them. It is a plan that they themselves have no input into. I didn't know how to communicate that I hated the pattern of my life. I hated it for a very long time. But how do you communicate this when the outside world sees you as completely successful and as someone who is doing all of the right things? How do you explain that being a practically straight A student and being gifted in every sport you play isn't what you want to do and doesn't make you happy? They would have had my head examined. Funny, maybe they should have. They would have found out that I was very depressed and didn't want to continue living. Sometimes kids like me feel so lost, but the outside world cannot see this. If we are caught drinking, they either cover it up or slap us on the wrist. Don't you understand it is a cry for help? The drinking is a guise to cover up the pain. Kids like me can be pretty quiet because we are afraid if we start talking we will reveal our internal thoughts to the outside world.

I have to stop for a minute and say something really important, "Hi Mom and Dad, I love you so much! I am so sorry that I did this to myself and to our family. Please forgive me. It wasn't you, it was nothing you did or didn't do. It was nothing you said or didn't say! It was me. I needed to learn to speak up for myself and stand up for my own belief system. I couldn't do that. Dad, you helped so many kids just like me, so I know this has been extra hard on you. Please stop asking yourself why you did not see this coming and how you did not know. You couldn't have known, Dad. I was really good at hiding my feelings and truths. I observed the other kids you helped for years so I knew exactly what not to say or do to send off any signals. Mom, you are the most gentle and kind soul that I have ever met and I will be eternally grateful to you for all of the love and support you provided to me. I know it must be hard on you because I did talk to you so much. You are a great listener. I was always aware not to reveal my deepest secrets. Society doesn't currently support going in your own direction or making your own path. That is starting to shift right now. That is part of what I have been working on since I left the Earth. I help others to find their love and passion and to listen to their truth. I am proud of that. Just know that we are and continue to be connected in a way that is much more powerful than in human terms. I will not leave you; it only appears that I did. I love you the most! Lou (not my real name, but you will know me anyway.)"

Lou's Life Lesson:

My life lesson was to "listen". I did a lot of listening when I was on Earth. I listened to my teachers, my coaches, and the adults in my life. I even listened to some other teenagers, but that is not the listening I am speaking about now. I am speaking about listening to myself, the self that lays deep within me, the self in my soul, the one I never really took the time to get to know that well. That is where my truth lays and that is where your truth is. Find it before it is too late. If you are too busy trying to please everyone else and trying to fulfill all of their demands, you will never find your own truth. You will end up feeling very worn down. Why wouldn't this wear you down? You are fighting against the tide. I practice listening every day now and I have become a lot stronger and connected to myself because of this. It takes a lot of practice to enter into this state. When you begin you may experience fear, as you never know what the results will be once you follow your own guidance. It is the unknown and it can leave you unsettled. Most people are so programmed to follow someone else's instructions or directions that they feel lost when they are left with their own thoughts and their own choices. Imagine feeling alone because you are left with your own thoughts? Just the opposite is actually true, you just don't know this yet. When you spend time alone listening to your own guidance, it builds a sense of self-worth, a sense of self-trust. There is nothing more powerful than this, especially if you take the time to document the guidance you receive. This documentation will become your "truth" and your proof that this method actually works. You will be able to validate each guidance you receive as it occurs. Just be sure to date the guidance you receive, so that you can't talk yourself out of it afterwards. If you don't take the time to document your guidance, your mind will play tricks on you and try to make you believe you documented the guidance after the event occurs. If you date your documented guidance, you will have the proof that you need and it will help you to start believing in yourself.

By the way, if I stuck it out, I would have wanted to do something in the field of science with testing these theories and developing new ways of thinking and learning for people. It would have been tedious and taken a lot of patience, but I would have been excited about doing it. It would have been something on the cutting edge that people wouldn't necessarily understand in the beginning, but they didn't understand my way of thinking on Earth either and look where that got me. By the way, I am doing this work now and you are already seeing the results of it. Each time there is a thought shift or someone else feels that light go off inside of themselves it means one of my theories is working. I help to create miracles every day. My mission now is to get individuals to believe in themselves even when the outside world doesn't comply. This will change the world and you will see more "common" type people becoming successful, because they will start to be valued by society as they value themselves. Wouldn't that be a nice change?

Thank you for taking the time to listen to this important message. I wish I understood this information in detail when I was alive on Earth, but I am excited that I am part of this complete transformation that is now taking place on Earth. You are part of this change and your life will get better with each passing day. Just quiet your mind and listen to your true guidance, there is a lot of information that you haven't even tapped into yet. Don't take the easy way out. It turns out that it is not the easy way. Seeing your parents, your siblings, your friends and even some of your teachers who you thought didn't like you grieve and suffer every day is more painful than anything that I ever experienced on Earth. The difference is you can't comfort them. They can't see or hear you or feel your warm touch. Humans have a lot more going for them than they can even begin to realize. Embrace your existing situation with love and hope and the rest will fall into place. You don't have to be happy every day. You just have to take some positive steps to finding your peace and happiness. Each steps helps to build the next until you are the one teaching or helping others to find their own truth. You will be blessed believe me, just wait and see! Lou

CHAPTER XXI
Hello my name is Joey

I hung myself in my closet. What a stupid decision that was. It was completely devastating for my family. My parents still cannot speak about it even after over thirty years. It was really a hateful thing to do. I am here to talk to the youth. Please listen to my message, it is important. Nothing you can do is worth taking your own life. Everything, and I mean everything, can be corrected through a different action or direction. I am not saying you won't have to own up or pay up for your direct actions. I am saying that it is possible to turn around anything as long as you learn your lesson from your decided action.

Sometimes things seemed so "BIG" and blown up that they appeared to be irreparable, but I have since learned it is all relative to what you measure it against. I can honestly say now, that if something devastating happened to one of my brothers, then my situation would have become so small and insignificant in comparison. The problem is, I couldn't see that at the time. Instead, I thought my situation was the end of the world. I thought my dad would kill me and that my mom would never want to look at me again. I took the cowardly way out. It did not benefit anyone. When you are my age, you really do not comprehend that your decisions are final and there is no turning back. You think you understand this, but believe me when I tell you that you don't. I tried for several years following my death to get back into a human body so I could redo everything and be with my family during this painful and terrible time. That is not possible. I made the decision to leave. Once I made that decision and I was gone, no longer in my body, that is when it hit me hard. This is no game. You do not get to come back. Not in the form that you were in when you left. You can send signs and hang around your family and friends. Some people on Earth even feel you and know you are around them. Even with that knowledge it is hard to deal with. It is hard for me too!

I want to be able to talk to you, to hold you, to hug you. I want to tell you "I love you." It is frustrating that you cannot hear me. So, instead I send messages through the animals and other people. I try my hardest to let you know that I am still very much alive and well. I hope you know this and that you are aware enough to receive my messages. Sometimes, I don't think you receive them because you keep asking me the same questions over and over again when I have already answered you. Then again, I guess you did that when I was on Earth too so maybe that is my validation. Ha! I just made myself laugh! Anyway, let me get back to why I am here and what I would like to share with you.

Joey's Life Lesson:

My life lesson was to listen to my own voice and mind. I was tricked. I dated someone who was sooooo in love with me, So she said. But here is the part of my life lesson that I want you to know more than anything else. Someone does not love you if they have to try to possess you or if they try to trick you into being with them. This is called possessiveness. This is called insecurity. This is called jealousy. And, this is called control in the unhealthiest manner. If someone loves you, they respect you and your wishes. They want you to grow and follow your own dreams. They get excited for you when something good happens to you even if it does not involve them. That is why it is really difficult to find true love on Earth. Most humans are too self absorbed and they want you to love them more than they want to love you. Here is another point about love. Love has to be selfless. Yes,

116

completely selfless. Be a good listener and don't give advice unless you are asked for it. Be supportive and believe in the person you love no matter what. Don't dump your fears and beliefs on them. They need to have your support and love no matter what. If everyone loved like this the divorce rate would drop significantly. So don't let someone talk you into marrying them, or trick you by saying they are "pregnant". Even if that were true, you get to decide. It is your life! Your decision to be a good father is already decided and there is no turning back on that. But the decision to get married is all yours and you get to decide. By the way, when you do become a parent, the amount of love you receive from that child will be far more than the love you will provide. Yes, there will be stages in the child's life where you will not believe this to be true. That will pass and you will be rewarded for all of the love that you provided.

To the youth, please believe in yourself first. Be happy with your accomplishments, and don't let all of those other voices get in your head and convince you that you are not worthy or motivated enough. Those voices never help you do more. They only make you angry and in most cases make you turn the other way. They will restrict you by locking you into fear so that you cannot move forward in any aspect of your life. If you practice believing in yourself, you will become successful. You will be happy and you will make good choices. It is not that you can't ask for guidance or support. It is just that you are the one who has to make the ultimate decision for yourself. I am talking to the 17 plus generation. If you don't learn to make decisions and learn the results of those decisions by yourself, you will always doubt yourself and be looking to others to tell you which direction to go to next. This is the quick road to depression and disaster. Trust your own instincts. Listen to yourself, not your friends or their friends. Just believe in you.

Here is another part of my life lesson that I would like to share with you. Become a very good listener at a very young age. Talk less and listen more. As you do this you will gain so much knowledge. You will learn to process all of this information during your own quiet time and you will be able to make more accurate and better choices for yourself. If you are always thinking about what to say or what advice to give when you are suppose to be listening, then you will miss so much valuable information. Honestly, this is the quickest way to learn. When you really stay present and listen you gain better control of your own reactions, thoughts, and feelings. It helps you to grow into a very strong person. You will learn to gain trust in yourself, which is all you really need. If you have trust in yourself, you become unstoppable. Then anything that happens to you never leads to you feeling like you have to end your life to get out of a situation. Instead you will know that you have choices and different options or directions that you can take. This is very empowering.

What a waste for me. I was just about to start the best part of my life and I threw it all away. You may not realize this, but being in human form is such an honor. Believe me, I love being on the other side. There are some great advantages here, but being a human is simply amazing. The things you can do and feel. How you can touch anything you want, you can smell the sweet scent of Earth, how you can see every aspect of the world. How you can cry when you are sad and laugh when you are happy!

Human emotions are a gift. Even the sad ones. I miss that. I miss you being able to hear me and see me. I miss you hugging me. I miss us having a good old fashion conversation about sports or cars or anything that we would love to compete about. That's another thing I miss, competing with you. Brotherly love, there is nothing like that here! I love how you have honored me and became such an honorable man! I love you Bro! Yes, I am here and very much alive, just please stop asking me the same questions over and over again. Now, read my story again, because you have a lot more to accomplish in your life and only you can make the decision to do this. Don't keep asking others for their advice. They are limited in their knowledge. You know what is best for you, but you have to believe in yourself and stop worrying about what others will think or say about it. It is not their life, it is yours! I love you with my full heart and soul! Joey!

P.S. I love the lake thing! That is ideal!

Believe In Your Truth

CHAPTER XXII
Hello my name is Angel

I died when I was seven and a half years old. When you are as young as I was you are proud of being a half of year older so you always describe your age as the number you are, and then you say and a half. I was still in first grade. I got sick in kindergarten. Actually, that is when my family found out that I was sick. I never really felt good. I was a whiny little kid and always in some sort of pain. It got worse when I went to school. I didn't have the ability to fight off infections, so when I went to school things got worse for me. There was a time when my family and teachers thought I was just trying to seek attention, somewhere around the age of four, when I should have been becoming a BIG girl. It wasn't for attention. It was just that my sickness was inside of me and you couldn't really see it and I couldn't really describe it other than always saying I didn't feel good in my belly area. I had the most beautiful baby blue eyes and curly blond hair, the fluffy soft long curls that people always want to touch when they walk by you. My mother named me right. Everyone always said that I looked like an angel, even though I was never really happy. It is tough to be happy when your body never feels good. My mom used to say that when I smiled I could light up the whole world. I was full of sunshine. The times that I was the happiest was when I was outside planting or playing in the flowers. I loved everything about the outdoors. It was the one time that I could forget about my pain. It is when I would sing and play like a normal child. Do you know what it is like to be in pain and not feel good anytime and to have no one believe or to know how to help you? It is exhausting. When I was really little,

I didn't even enjoy being held by my own parents. I was born with my disease and here's the thing. It wasn't anyone's fault. My mom didn't do anything wrong while she was carrying me. It just happened.

My skin was sensitive and my belly hurt all of the time. Sometimes it would get so extended. My mom took me to the doctors many times but they could never find anything wrong with me. To be honest with you they didn't look too deep. I looked like a healthy little angel on the outside, so they did the usual testing and nothing would show up. After awhile I could sense that the people around me just thought I was making it up. After a while I would just become extremely quiet, as I understood not to say my belly hurt. I didn't like to eat, but I did like to drink. That is probably because I couldn't digest my food, which is why my belly hurt all of the time. I guess none of this is important now but it is important for one reason...

I think parents and teachers should do a better job of really listening to children. Children don't usually lie. They are actually pretty truthful. I know some kids can lie but if a child keeps saying the same thing over and over again, then you should really pay attention to them. Even if the message doesn't make sense to you. It is really hard being a child. You don't get to express yourself. You are asked to be quiet all of the time when all you want to do is talk. It is also very hard for us little guys to sit in that hard wooden chair all day without moving or talking. You should try it sometime, you won't last more than two hours. We need to be moving and learning in a fun and creative way. The best way to teach us is through music and movement. We love to move and talk. If you let us express ourselves it would be so much better for everyone. We can't be quiet for six hours a day. Our brains get tired that way. We can't absorb your words for that long either.

You know when a child dies the world stops. People that didn't even know me cried. I know my friends, teachers, aunt and uncles, my parents and siblings would do anything to hear me speak again or laugh. They would probably even be excited to hear me cry or complain about my stomachaches. They can't. Sometimes I crawl into bed with my parents at night. I know my momma feels me. They both miss me so much. I like the fact that I can sneak in their bed at night and they can't get mad at me and say, "You are a big girl now, you need to sleep in your own bed." Now if they knew I was in their bed they wouldn't mind at all. They would be happy.

Angel's Message:

I came to tell you that children are fragile. They need to be handled with care. Don't wait until something happens to them to understand this. Did you ever go up to an angry child and rub their back? Just that one gesture can change everything. I wish someone could have listened to me sooner, but I was just a little kid who didn't know how to communicate more than saying "my belly hurts" over and over again. I don't blame my parents or anyone else. I was not supposed to be on Earth for very long. To be honest with you, I couldn't have tolerated it. I was so sensitive on every level. My skin hurt if you touched it. My belly hurt every day. I could feel everything around me. It was very uncomfortable. I only felt good when I was outside. When you go to school you don't get to spend much time outside. You are inside most of the time. I want to help other children. I am helping on the other side with all of the educators and musicians here. I help to develop fun games and activities that will help the children on Earth to learn in a more creative and interesting way.

The children of today's generation will not learn the archaic way they are being taught. They are too sensory and need to learn through touch and feeling, more hands on. We are very far away from that actually happening though. Some of the newer teachers are already shifting this paradigm. It will be a whole new world of learning. The exciting part is the jobs that these children will do when they grow up haven't even been invented yet. They will go to school for things they really love learning about and turn it into a profitable business that will benefit the world. Things are not getting worse as many of you say. They are getting better and more exciting. I love it here. I am surrounded by the other children here and I experience more love than I ever could have imagined. When I miss my family I visit them.

I am happy and I do not have any pain or discomfort here. All of the children here are happy. They play and sing every day. The ones that couldn't walk can run here. It is a beautiful peaceful place and there are lots of beautiful flowers. I love everything about it. The best part is that it is completely safe here and you never have to worry about getting hurt. Please know that I am safe, happy, and well cared for!

Your littlest Angel!

CHAPTER XXIII
Hello my name is Steve

I lived near a lake. I love the peace and calm quiet of being near water. I don't think people realize the massive significance of water. It is one of the most important resources to ensure you continue to live. It is the one thing that really cleanses your body. Some people use it as a blessing tool. You can't cook without it and it would be really hard to eat without it to wash down your food. It even cleanses the Earth, feeds the flowers, the plants, and the trees. Water fills our oceans, rivers, lakes, and streams. You use it to wash your car. Your pet can't live without it. Believe it or not, it even cleanses your soul. Do you ever just stop and really just connect with the sound of cleansing rain? It is such a beautiful sound. How about listening to a rapidly running river as it flows by?

Did you know that one drop of water continually dripping over time will develop a crevice in the hardest of stones? It is pure and simple. That is what I want to speak to you about. It is time to get back to the pure and simple things in your life. This is one of the keys to happiness. When I was here on Earth I was not as aware of all of the benefits of water. Yes, I liked the look of it, and I loved being around it, but I was too busy getting things done. I spent more hours in the office thinking, analyzing and creating than I ever did outside enjoying the beauty and miracles of the Earth. I had acquired a lot of things. Although it was nice, I now realize that my focus should have been more on the natural resources available here on Earth. We don't need more electronics. We have what we need now. Think about it. You can be at work sitting at your desk and without moving you can check the weather, catch up on the news, and order a new outfit to wear that weekend. You can check and pay your bills. You can learn about anything in the world you can think of. It has gotten to the point where you don't even have to type it. You can just ask "Siri." She will tell you whatever it is that you need or want to know.

If I could do my life all over again, I would spend as much time with water as I could. I would use that same intelligence that I was born with and apply it to figuring out a way to get fresh clean water to every part of the world. I would figure out a way to have back up clean fresh water available for any area of the world in the event of a disaster so everyone could meet their basic needs of staying hydrated and cleansing their bodies. It is ironic that I spent my entire career focused on electronics. Electronics and water are not a good combination. It is a very dangerous combination, so you have to choose one. I chose electronics in my lifetime on Earth and now I am choosing water and will continue to do so until every living being has access and enough good, clean, pure, and refreshing water to live on. It makes sense, you need water to grow apples right?

I wasted way too much of my life working and thinking and not enough time barefoot and enjoying my beautiful wife and family. I would change that too. My wife misses me, but she was so used to me always working, her transition was easier. I acted like a dead person when I was alive and now that I am dead I feel very much alive. The people in my life can easily pretend I am at work and they can carry on with their day. I know there are certain days that this won't work and the grief will hit them hard, but I am the one who is grieving. I was blessed with so many amazing tools, and I wasted a lot of them cramped in office space coming up with new plans and ideas that had very little to do with the precious Earth.

Now I look around at Earth and see all the amazing things that I never took the time to embrace or even notice while I was there. I had all of the money in the world. I could have done anything that I wanted to. I made more in one year than most people make in their entire career. I wouldn't consider myself a material person, but I certainly could have used some of the money to travel to places to enjoy the peace and beauty of the Earth. I could have used some of that money to help those who were less fortunate. That is what I would do differently. I would travel to various places in the world and work toward getting running water to every family I encountered. Then I would rest and enjoy the beauty of their land surrounded by delicious nature. My wife would laugh at me if she knew this and ask me if I was feeling OK. I don't actually believe she would think it is I, but it is me. I am transformed.

When you use your mind every day such as I did, you get caught into a whirlwind of thought and activity. Even when you get home, you can't get your mind to slow down or stop. I would wake up in the middle of the night with ideas floating through my head and I would have to write them down. If only I could have been a little more connected to nature to really get that gifted creativity I was born with to work to benefit Mother Nature.

I was relatively young when I died. I say relatively because it is all relative to whomever you are speaking to. I was in my young fifties. Do you know that most people didn't really care for me before I died? I had either ignored them or turned them away. When you have the success that I had and the amount of thoughts going through your brain, it starts out with you just not noticing those around you. You don't even hear them when they say good morning to you. Then they just stop speaking to you all together. At first you don't really notice, then one day you notice how people look at you and almost shun away from you when they see you coming. They are intimidated by you, or they simply don't know how to hold a conversation with you. They think you are too intelligent, so they are afraid to hold a conversation with you. As a human you need to interact with other people. It helps to nourish your soul. Never be too busy to connect with other people. This is a sure way to create an early death. Your soul, your body, and your mind all need interaction with other people. Here is something else you probably don't know. You can't be more intelligent than someone else. Everyone has their own gifts and something unique to offer this world. This is intelligence. If I was so intelligent, why did I waste so much time closed up in an office by myself. Why did I neglect my precious family? Why didn't I notice all of the beautiful things on Earth? That is not intelligence, that is ignorance. I made more money than most people will ever dream of, but if I could do it all over again I would stick with the basics. The money couldn't buy me more time. It didn't bring me happiness. It certainly didn't buy me self-worthiness, which is something I lacked my whole life. That is what my "success" was rooted in. I wanted to build myself into something worthy, something meaningful. The more I built, the less worth I felt. It is a secret I kept locked deep inside of myself. I never got over being rejected as a small infant. Even though I couldn't remember it, I could feel it deep inside of myself. I found out through years of relentlessly working toward one success after another that no amount of money could make you feel what you don't feel inside of yourself.

Fast forward, now that I am here, I can see that it was the simple and basic things in life that would have brought me my self-worthiness. The more I connected with people and nature, the more I would have discovered how special and unique I was. I would have been able to accept myself and realized that I could have mentored and helped others do the same. I could have invested my time and energy in giving more back to my community and I would have forgotten all about my own problems and issues. I couldn't even teach my own children to have self-confidence because I didn't know how to example this for them. Instead, I drove them to be successful on their own. I should have spent every free second I had with them. I should have taken them camping and taught them about living and connecting to nature. That is the best part of being here. You are connected every second. You don't even have to think about it. It is all around you and inside of you. You just become it. I have found my peace and happiness. I am sticking with my commitment. I am going to figure out a way to bring fresh clean water to every family so they can meet their basic needs and survive. I am more alive now than I ever was on Earth.

Tomorrow when you wake up, before you do anything else, step outside and breath some fresh air into your lungs. Have a cold delicious drink of water and thank God for every person you cross paths with during your day. Look those people in the eye and genuinely know that you are happy that they are in your life. Be completely embraced in every moment and spend more of those moments in happy times than in robotic motions. Be alive and live well. Meet your dreams, but choose your dreams carefully. With much love and compassion. Steve!

CHAPTER XXIV
Hello my name is D.

I guess I am the last one, for this book anyway. I had no idea I was going to step forward to share my story with you. My friends and family here encouraged me to do so. It is hard for me. I am very shy and quiet, but at the same time personable. I had two sides. I had the confident cop side that was strong and resilient. I loved working with the kids. If I could make a difference in a kid's life, then I would go out of my way to make that happen, whether I was on duty or not. I have always loved kids. I did not have any of my own. I was married. My community was my family. They loved me and I loved them. On the other side of my personality I was painfully shy. I was filled with insecurity and shame. I didn't really show this to too many people, but those that knew me well knew that side of me existed. I did not have a mean bone in my body. It is actually amazing to me that I became a cop. I followed in my family's footsteps.

I wanted to honor my late brother, who I adored and loved more than anything on this Earth. He was an amazing person. He was much more outgoing than I was. He had another side too, and that was depression. He tried to keep it well hidden but he couldn't hide it from me. We shared a room together when we were kids, maybe that is why I could read his every thought before he even spoke the words. The day he took his own life was the worst day of my life. My heart cracked that day, and it was never the same after that. I went through the motions for months with little memory of what happened on a daily basis. I poured my heart and soul into helping the kids in the community. My brother was taking medication to help him, but he took it too far. I was dedicated to making sure that kids could have a mentor to look up to, someone to confide in, and someone to support them and keep them away from drugs and alcohol. I saved a lot of kids and redirected them. They were like my own sons and daughters. Every time they saw me coming they would smile and come running toward me to say hello. It made my heart swell.

I had a secret locked deep inside myself that only a few people knew about. I can't actually even say they knew. They suspected and thought they knew my secret, but honestly they didn't. I would never admit what happened, I took it to my grave with me. I came from a very strict religious family. You were raised a certain way and that is the way it was. You didn't discuss your feelings; you just did what you knew you were supposed to do. I followed all the proper channels. Even graduated at the top of my class. I was a Class A citizen on all levels. I got married and appeared to have a very normal life, but that deep dark secret was always lingering buried deep inside of me. It was there every day. The only thing that felt worse was the hole in my heart from my brother's death. Now I knew that he knew my secret. Turns out he had the same secret that I did.

My dad was of a militant style, so there was no way I was going to admit this while he was still on this Earth. That meant I couldn't even tell my mom, because she was from the old school and I knew even if she promised me she would feel obligated to tell my dad. If I was young enough, I imagined he would beat me thinking he could get me to wise up. I tried to be perfect on every other level to make up for this major flaw I felt I had. I would spend an hour polishing my shoes before work. I would make sure my uniform was crisp. I even made sure my gun was clean. Every step I took was calculated with thought and consideration. The only thing you couldn't see by looking at me was my broken heart and soul. The only person on Earth who I thought I could turn to left me abruptly. My pain grew by the day. I dealt with it by becoming kinder to anyone I crossed paths with. I thought if I could say a kind word or do a kind deed for someone it would relieve my pain.

Here is something you may not know. When you are a "gay" man, it is possible to completely love a woman. You love her with your entire heart and soul, but you cannot give her the full package. Women are smart and they figure these things out. At first they blame themselves, thinking they are not attractive. My wife was one of the most beautiful women I have ever laid eyes on. I loved her every day of my life since I met her. As we got further into our marriage, we grew further apart. I knew she loved me, too, and that she was very proud of what an honorable man I was. It is just that when you cannot share your humanness with the woman you love, she grows restless and frustrated, especially if you don't have the ability to talk about it and give her a reason why.

It took my wife twenty years to build up the courage to ask me if I was gay. I remember the words coming out of her mouth and how it felt like I had just been shot in the heart. I knew I was "gay". I had known for a very long time, but to hear those words spoken by the women you love, well, I can't really explain it, but it shocks your system. Like you are going to be found out. Your biggest fear and insecurity is getting revealed right in front of you. Your head swirls in a hundred different directions. Who will she tell? Will the community still love me and look up to me? What if my father finds out? Wow! I can't even process that one. I admitted to my wife that night that I was "gay". We cried together for several hours. My wife had so many questions. I couldn't believe she could have stored up all of those questions for so many years. Every type of emotion you can imagine went through us. My wife felt deceived. For twenty years she thought there was something wrong with her. She felt like I lied to her and cheated her out of experiencing motherhood. Every fear I could ever have imagined came through me too, until I asked the dreaded question, "Are you going to leave me?" She didn't answer me right away. Then I heard her whisper that she would have to think about it. She had a lot to process. I knew at that very moment that she would leave me and my life would never be the same. How was I going to function in the community that I loved and that loved me as a single "gay" man, when I was known as lovable D., the clean cut, kind and happy married man? I felt a thousand pounds of weight crushing in on my chest cavity. We both cried until we fell asleep.

I knew when I woke up in the morning that I was going to make the same choice my brother had made. I did not see a reason to continue on with my life and part of me was thinking (not very clearly I admit now) that I would save my wife the embarrassment of having to divorce me and having my deep dark secret revealed to the world, bringing her even more embarrassment. I reasoned that this way, she would be a grieving widow and eventually she would marry someone who could fulfill all of her needs and wishes. It took me a few days to plan everything out. I never actually considered changing my mind. I only knew my life the way it was. It was safe and clean and routine. I liked that. I didn't want to deal with the course change that was about to begin.

The day I died was a beautiful sunny day. It seemed like everyone I met was extra happy and beautiful to me. I now understand that this is because I was seeing things in the truth for the very first time in my life, but I didn't know this at the time. You can't even imagine what goes through your mind when you make this decision, especially being raised in such a strict religious family. I figured I would never get to see my brother again because we would both be going to "hell". That is what we were taught in our religious school. I leave the actual religion name out because there is no purpose in bringing any blame. There is nothing and no one to blame. As I know others have pointed out in this book, you are solely responsible for your own life decisions and choices. I made the decision to end my life and I can tell you now that it was not a good one. I chose my home as my place of departure. What a stupid idea that was. My wife is the one who found me. Like I didn't put her through enough pain and sorrow over the years. When you make a decision like this you don't think clearly. Even though you think you are planning everything out, that is so far from being true. I actually went to work out earlier that day. That was part of my daily routine. This is proof that you don't think clearly. I was worried about getting in my daily workout routine so that I could take care of the body that I was about to damage. Foolish! I drank my favorite cup of coffee. I even did my community rounds. The whole time putting off in my mind what I knew was going to happen at the end of the day.

I liked routine. It made everything seem normal and safe. I am not going to describe my death. It was a stupid thing to do and I am not proud of it. I caused excruciating pain to more people than I ever could have imagined. Grown men were brought to their knees from the suffocation they felt in their hearts. "I am very sorry! Very very sorry. I was a coward." I knew you loved me, but I wasn't thinking about this because I didn't love myself. I tried to take the best corrective actions I could to fix this insecurity problem, but it never really went away. I broke my wife's heart in half. I will never forgive myself for that. Not that this matters now, but my wife during those few days decided she wouldn't leave me because she loved me too much. Imagine that? She didn't get the chance to tell me that. It wouldn't have mattered. I couldn't give her the one thing a husband should provide for his wife and she loved me more and wanted me in her life. When I tell you that this is breaking my heart just writing these words, it is. It is so painful to know that so many people can love you more than you can love yourself. What is worse is, if you make the decision that I made, and then you will never get the chance to let them know how important they are to you. You lose that ability in an instant. That is all my death took was an instant. I actually put my slippers on just before. I wanted to be comfortable. Craziness! Do you realize that in that same instant it took me to put my slippers on, I could have made a different choice? I could have held my wife that very night and smelled the sweet scent of her hair as I fell asleep next to her beautiful body. I could have held her hand every day for the rest of my life.

I left my kids, every one of them. Every kid who looked up to me and relied on me to steer them in the right direction. I let them all down with no example of where to go from here. I left my precious goddaughter who needed me and everything I represented in her life. I left my aging mother who already had a broken heart. What kind of son does that to his own mother? I left my best friend who became my brother after my own brother died. I left a lot of gifts behind. It is painful even now to recount this and tell you my story. That is why I wasn't going to come through, but I had to. You have to give me this opportunity to redeem myself. I need to save at least one life. I have to help at least one person from making this type of decision. I am begging and pleading with you to please make a different choice. Find someone who can help you. I will help you. There were thousands of people affected by my death. People don't get over death by suicide. It is one of the most painful things a human will ever experience. They are laden with guilt and questions that never get answered. What could I have done to stop this? Does he know that I love him? What did I miss? Why did he leave me? Didn't he love me enough? Why? Why? Why?

Don't do this to your family and friends. Don't do this to your kids. They don't deserve it. It will build a sense of insecurity in them so deep you will never be able to break it down. The children take it the hardest. They truly believe they were not good enough. That you did not love them enough. Even if they were not your biological children, it will cut them like a knife. Tomorrow will be a better day. You just have to look for one small piece of hope or notice the tiniest miracle, like a new bud coming through the Earth after a long cold winter. There are people who will help you that you can trust. Love is solid. It is pure. People don't stop loving you because you are "gay" or for any other reason. Love is pure and infinite. There are people in every person's life that will love that person no matter what you say, do, or who you are. You need to know this and make a different choice. Do it for me. I can't take back my decision, but I work diligently every day to help "you" make a different choice than I did. I am here for you and I love you! You are worthy!

D.'s Life Message:

Please know that any children that have crossed since my time, I have been here to greet them. I help them with their transition and make them feel safe until they get comfortable with their new surroundings. You will be happy to know that I was greeted by my brother and we hugged like we have never seen each other before. We tell each other we love each other every day. There is no shame here. There is no judgment. I am at peace. I have been in school here learning to love and accept myself. This is something I have struggled with since I was a young boy. I practice saying positive things to myself every day and anyone new who arrives who has a self-confidence issue gets assigned to me so I can practice what I have learned and teach them the ropes. It is very fulfilling and rewarding.

Even though you may think once you cross into this place of peace and light that everything is all corrected, there is still a lot of work to be done. I am also working on forgiving myself for all of the pain that I have caused you; all of you that loved me, and all of you who never even met me but still loved me just based on what others told you about me. Each day gets easier and I make more progress. I have something important to share with you that I am pretty sure you have never heard before. When you grieve it is hard for us to forgive ourselves. I know I am crossing the line in asking for more than I have a right to here, but if you could honor our lives and share the positive and happy times you shared with us, it will help us to move into our own forgiveness and place of peace. Now I have something even bigger to ask you. CAN YOU PLEASE FORGIVE ME? Every single one of you. You too, Dad! I am so so so very sorry for being so cowardly. I would never make this choice again. NEVER! I can honestly say it is the absolute worst decision I ever made in my life. Please know that I work to extremes to help others on Earth to not make this same decision. It is a tough job, but I volunteered for the assignment because I will never forget that feeling of complete isolation and desolation I felt the second before. It is so painful. I am not speaking about the physical pain. I am talking about the immediate realization of what I just did and impact it is going to have on others. If you can forgive me, then it will help me to forgive myself and complete my assignment here. I hope you can feel the love I send down to you every day. You are always in my thoughts and prayers!

If it is OK, I would like to leave a few personal messages here:

To my beautiful, dedicated wife:

"I loved you with my whole heart and every aspect of my soul. I hope that is what you remember about me. I would have gone to the end of the Earth for you. I pray every day that you can forgive me for my actions and putting you in such a bad way. You are truly the best thing that ever happened to me on Earth. It is so important for me to tell you this, because you are the one I trusted the most. I am sorry I did not tell you the whole truth about myself. It had nothing to do with you. It was my own fear and insecurity, my own shame that was secretly stored deep inside of me for years. It was actually easier to just say I was "gay". I am so sorry for this decision. I love you more than the wind, the sun, the stars, and the moon. You are my everything. You are everything a man could ever ask for in a wife. I love the scent of your hair and I miss the warmth of your hand. It is time for you to allow your heart to heal. It is time for you to allow your heart to reopen and love again. It is time for you to move on from me. I know you loved me and accepted me with your whole heart. My only wish is for you to be happy and fulfilled in every way. He is coming. Please be open and don't let my deceit stop you from trusting and loving again. Your heart is too big to stay closed. I love you and you will feel me in the scent of the gentle breeze. You are the love of my life! Until we meet again! D."

To my Mom:

"Mom, it is so hard to write this to you. I can't even say the words, I am sorry, because they sound too shallow to me. So, instead, I am going to try to bring you the only gift I know how. Your two sons are together. We are closer than ever and we spend countless times talking about all the good memories we have from our childhood. You are a great mother. You did the best that you could and we love you for that. You are unique and that is what makes you the special women that you are. Mom, I will never forget all that you did for me. You are in my heart and soul. We will be connected forever. Not even death can separate a mother's love for her child and a child's love for their mother. I love you mom! We are safe and happy!"

To my sweet goddaughter:

"You are the joy of my life. You are the child I was never able to have on my own. You have to pick yourself up and keep moving. I know I did not mentor this to you by my terrible example. We are connected heart to heart and soul to soul. I am with you and I believe in you. Do not ever stop dreaming and moving toward the life that you want. It is time to start finding joy and happiness in every day. You are beautiful, talented, and stronger than you think. Bad things don't happen. You are just noticing the bad things. You need to look toward the sky and notice all of the miracles. I know you can hear me in your mind. Now, listen and move ahead. It is time for you to make some life choices that will bring your life joy and happiness. Don't stay hidden. I did that and it didn't help me. You are going to be better than me. Make me proud of you. Be all that you can be. I won't let you stay where you currently are. It is not serving you well and you are making your parents worry sick. Pick up the ball and keep moving kid. I love you! Listen to your heart! You will be pleasantly surprised."

To my best friend:

"Thank you! Thank you, for believing in me when I couldn't even believe in myself. Thank you for helping me during some of the darkest times in my life. Thank you for letting me share in some of the greatest moments of your life. My goddaughter. You gave me a gift that I couldn't even give to myself. Thank you for mentoring me, caring for me, and looking out for me. Thank you for always having my back. Thank you for listening to me and hearing my words even when I couldn't speak them. You are the greatest brother I could ask for (no offense to my own brothers).

I will leave you with this message, live your life to the fullest every day. Don't look backwards. If something is going against you, know that it means there is a blessing coming right around the corner. Don't despair. Life can be so much lighter and enjoyable if you just notice and act alive."

Message to the youth:

"To the youth, make good clean choices. Those quick fixes will lead you down the wrong dark path. Choose something that brings you closer to your goals and dreams. Alter your goals and dreams as you grow and learn. It is never too late to make a different choice! Do something kind for someone else every day. It will make you a better person. Even when you don't feel like it, do it anyway.

I send you all love from the deepest part of my heart and soul! We are connected soul to soul. D."

P.S. By the way, I took my deep dark secret to my grave with me. I found out when I got here that my brother had the same secret. Here is something you should know. If someone has a drastic change in their personality or disposition, look deeper. It is not a coincidence. You can make a difference, just never give up trying. The ones who are more distant need the love, patience, and kindness more.

Message from Author:

Remember my first grade teacher? Her name was Sister Annine. One of my favorite cousins, who is a year younger than me, told me the other day that when she was in first grade she wrote a sentence on a paper that said "I Love God." She brought it up to Sister Annine to review and Sister Annie stated that this sentence was too simple and my cousin Patty would have to do something else. My cousin was devastated. She was six years old.

One of the greatest things I have learned in doing this work is that saying those three simple words, "I Love God," is the quickest and simplest way to manifest the life that you want and desire. Letting God know that you love him is more important than anything else you will do on this Earth. It is the secret pathway to all of your happiness and life's true path. That is right Sister Annine, "It is simple, but it is the simple that is perfect."

Love God, your life, the universe, and everything in between.

Expect a miracle, because it is on its way!

In the brightest light, Maureen.

SUMMARY
The Author's Story

T his is a story that I have never shared with anyone. Not in its entirety like I am going to do here. It was a beautiful spring day in April 2009. I was working in Corporate America in a very stressful financial job. I woke early and was on the road to work by 7:00 a.m. I had some important deadlines to meet and even though I hadn't arrived home the night before until 11:00 p.m., I knew I had to get an early start on the day if I was going to meet my deadlines.

I arrived at work and started my work. I worked straight through until 7:30 p.m. I was done and I was so excited that I was going to make it home to see my husband and girls before they went to bed. I realized I hadn't seen my daughters in several days. Right after I had that thought my office phone rang. I was tempted not to answer it, but I did. As I lifted the receiver I heard that little voice in the back of my mind letting me know that I had just made a big mistake. On the other end of the phone was a whole panel of executives requesting an emergency conference call at 8:00 p.m. that evening. They wanted to make sure I would be on that call. I heard myself say, "Yes, I will be there." I hung up knowing that something was very very wrong with my life.

I was happily married and was blessed after many years with three beautiful daughters. Every night when I arrived home no matter what time it was, my husband had my dinner wrapped and ready for me. The house was clean, if it was too late for him to see me, he would leave me a note of encouragement or love. I lived in a safe community in a beautiful home. I was very well educated. On the outside my life appeared picture perfect.

I decided to stay at the office to take the conference call at 8:00 p.m.; I decided it would not be good to be driving on the highway while taking notes from the call. I dialed in at 8:00 p.m. and I was assigned an emergency financial project that was to be presented to an executive team in Boston, MA, at 10:00 a.m. the next morning. I had just completed a twelve-hour project and my entire body and mind were completely spent. I hung up the phone and cried.

I sat at my desk and felt completely lost. I did not have any food with me. I hadn't eaten in several hours. I was exhausted and I just wanted to go home and see my family. The next thing that happened was surreal. I heard a tapping on my office window. My office was beautiful and had a huge glass window that faced a wooded lot. It was just starting to get dark. I looked up at the window and I saw a beautiful yellow bird just tapping on the window. I don't remember what kind of bird it was; I just remember the beautiful shade of yellow. I just stopped and watched it for five minutes as it fluttered its wings and tapped on my window. I understood it to be a message. I knew what I had to do. I had to tap into my intuitive gifts to get this project complete and delivered on time.

I started the project at 8:30 p.m. that night and I completed it at 12:30 a.m. I sent the information out to the executive team and got into my car to drive home. I was passing through Providence RI at 1:00 a.m. as I heard my blackberry dinging. Each time I heard that sound I cringed. I was thinking I should not be driving through Providence, RI, at 1:00 a.m., by myself. I just started crying and begging God to just end my life. I told him I didn't want to be here anymore. I was too tired and I couldn't keep on the path I was on, but I didn't know how to get off that path. Everyone on the outside viewed me as a complete success. I viewed myself as a complete failure. I was not living the life that I desired and I was completely out of balance.

I noticed a sharp bend in the road with a cement wall. I decided I was just going to crash my car directly into the wall. I reasoned that no one would ever know it was intentional. I had been working 60-70 hour weeks and everyone in my life knew I was exhausted. They would have believed I just feel asleep behind the wheel. I had the perfect solution. I just wanted this pain and vicious cycle to end.

Within a second of making that decision a small white car came out of nowhere. I had just looked into my rear view mirror and no one else was on the highway with me. This small white car came flying at me right to my bumper. I remember feeling a cold breeze blow my hair and the hair on my arms stood up on end even though all of the windows in the car were closed. I remember yelling, "No, God! I don't want to die, I want to live!" At the very second the small white car swerved around me. I blinked my eyes and when I looked ahead there was no car to be seen anywhere. It was like the car disappeared. I couldn't believe it! To this day I believe that car was an angel interceding on my behalf, making me understand the value of my life. You can't just give your value away! I was here to serve a purpose and I had to start doing that every single day!

Author's Life Lesson:

My miracle was that I realized in that tiny little second that I wanted to live more than anything in this world. I wanted to go home and be with my family. I wanted this vicious cycle to end, so that I had full control over my life decisions and choices.

No one owns you! No one makes your choices for you! You do! After that night I could only see the miracle in every person's eyes. I could only see the miracle in every situation. I was always in full control. I did not have to take the phone call that night. I could have said "No" to the assignment. I should have done that a long time ago.

The end of the story is that I delivered that presentation the next morning in Boston at 10:00 a.m. I had gotten three hours of sleep the night before. Before I presented, I asked the angels to dress me, I asked the saints and my grandparents to assist me, and I asked Mother Mary to speak through me. At the end of the presentation, one of the top executives pulled me aside and said he was very impressed and he couldn't believe I was able to pull it all together in such a short time! I remember saying words I didn't even know the meaning to. They just came out of me. I had to lookup the words after the meeting and they were right on point.

HaHa! I didn't do the work and the presentation, they did, all those who interceded on my behalf.

I ended my corporate career shortly after that in 2009. When I left Corporate America I was a senior vice president. A lot of people in my personal life saw my decision to end my career as a bad move. I heard things like "people would die to get a job like that." Guess what? That "golden" dream job almost ended my life. I guess you were right, but I am the decision maker and I am responsible for my life decisions.

My biggest life lesson has been to "Meet them where they are!" Don't try to sell them, convince them, negotiate with them, or bribe them. Just accept them for who they are and where they are on their own life path, even if it is a spouse, child, coworker, boss, or the store clerk who waits on you while you purchase your morning coffee. Greet everyone with complete acceptance and kindness. Take the time to be present and look each person in the eye. Ask them how they are doing. Take an interest. Sometimes that can be the one word or action that makes the difference in that person's day. That can be the shift in someone's day or your shift. It will be the first step to moving you in the right direction. It will give you purpose and stop you from just going through the motions.

My conclusion is that we have to start allowing each person to find his or her own true path from the very beginning. Do not try to condition or domesticate them into the path you believe will work for them. If you are not on your true path, you will struggle! If they are not on their own true path they will struggle and there is no greater pain than losing someone you truly love. So love them now, by allowing them to be what they came to be, not what you desire them to be.

The one thing that I find amazing every time I share messages with those who lost loved ones is that it is the tiny little things that they miss the most about the person they have lost. It is not the big major things. I never hear someone say, "I miss him getting straight A's, I miss my husband making six figures, I miss my daughter being the most popular one in her class." No, what I hear is "I miss the smell of her hair, I wish I could just get one more hug, I miss his smile, I miss the little annoying pranks he used to do, I miss the sound of his laughter." It is the uniqueness of the person that is missed the most, the things that no other human can duplicate.

Notice and value the lives right in front of you! Notice the miracles surrounding you each and everyday. Be diligent in honoring your true value.

FINAL NOTE FROM THE AUTHOR

Some of you may read this book and question whether these stories are true or not. Others may read these stories and question how I received all of these downloaded messages. The fact is I have never met any of the people in these stories with the exception of Alex. I do not know if the people in these stories used their real names or a pseudonym.. Some of them had me change their name several times. I cannot validate whether all of these details are accurate and true. The information just came in the form of downloaded messages and I wrote them down. My question to you is, "Does it really matter how I received these messages?" The real question is, isn't it time to remove the stigma of suicide and start valuing the life and miracles surrounding each and every one of us?

Every single day someone takes his or her own life. In that tiny defining moment a different choice could have been made. Because of that tiny defining moment, all of the surviving people are left with the realization and the impact of that individual's decision. Each individual life is valuable, no one more than another. Each person is special and unique and is needed here on this Earth.

If the individual messages in this book helps just one person to realize their true value or gets them to make a different choice, if just one person reading this book realizes why they are here and how they can make this world a better place, then this book will have served its' purpose.

You are here to love! You are here to value and honor yourself for your uniqueness. You are here to walk your own true path every day!
BELIEVE IN YOUR TRUTH!

Suicide Prevention

The National Suicide Prevention Lifeline
Is a 24-hour, toll-free, confidential suicide prevention hotline available to anyone in suicidal crisis or emotional distress.
www.suicidepreventionlifeline.org
1-800-273-TALK (8255)

The Samaritans
Mission is to reduce the incidence of suicide by alleviating despair, isolation, distress and suicidal feelings among individuals in our community, 24/7.
www.samaritanshope.org
(877) 870-4673 Call or Text

Crisis Text Line
Is the only 24/7, nationwide crisis-intervention text-message hotline.
www.crisistextline.org
press@crisistextline.org
Text the word "START" to 741-741

The Trevor Project
Is a nationwide organization that provide crisis intervention and suicide prevention services to lesbian, gay, bisexual, transgender and questioning.
www.thetrevorproject.org
(866) 488-7386
Text the word "Trevor" to 1-202-304-1200

Trans Lifeline
Is a nationwide toll-free crisis hotline staffed by and for transgender people.
www.translifeline.org
(877) 565-8860

ABOUT THE AUTHOR

Maureen Kayata worked successfully in Corporate America in the financial sector for over 25 years. She received her Bachelor of Science Degree from Salve Regina University in Newport, RI, and her MBA from Providence College in Providence, RI. She is the owner of Connections, which provides services for Hypnosis, Reiki, Reconnective Healing, The Reconnection, Angel Readings and Mediumship. Maureen also offers Business Coaching Sessions, to assist entrepreneurs to launch their successful business plans through a series of clear creative tools and guidance.

Maureen started receiving intuitive messages when she was six years old. These messages often acted as warnings in dangerous situations. Although Maureen never shared the messages with anyone during her young life, she always followed the guidance that she received. Her life was saved on multiple occasions because of these guided messages.

Maureen lives in New England with her husband of twenty-six years and her three beautiful daughters.

WWW.Connections.Solutions

www.ingramcontent.com/pod-product-compliance
Lightning Source LLC
LaVergne TN
LVHW021453080426
835509LV00018B/2260